Pilgrim Woman
Pilgrim Church

Maria Vlaemynck

Sheed & Ward

Sheed & Ward™ is a service of National Catholic Reporter Publishing Company, Inc.

Library of Congress Catalog Card Number: 91-61342

ISBN: 1-55612-456-2

Published by: Sheed & Ward
                115 E. Armour Blvd. P.O. Box 419492
                Kansas City, MO 64141-6492

To order, call: (800) 333-7373

Contents

To my granddaughter
Justine Marie

Chapter One
Adventure into New Territory

The small group of people on the bus began to grow noisier as they neared the city of Rotterdam and its harbor. It had been a long drive and someone, one of the cousins, suggested that they try a song. This gathering of relatives, young and old alike, some of whom had had little chance to travel before, had been eager to come along and see the newlyweds off on their journey to Canada. They were enjoying themselves, but their merriment was ill suited. I was beginning to feel the pangs of impending separation, now that I was about to board the ship and leave behind me all those who were dear.

I had felt brave that morning, rising at 4:00 to join this noisy group of well-wishers on a four-hour bus ride to Rotterdam. I had said my good-byes to my mom and the others who could not come to see me off. My mother was pregnant with her thirteenth child, and my last words to her had been words of encouragement and comfort. But now I began to feel a stifling sadness about the final moment of separation. Sitting beside my father, who was clutching my hand in his, and nodding my head in the direction of the singers, I said, "Are they crazy!" My father was close to tears, and he struggled angrily to maintain control. "I wish they would keep quiet," he answered, hugging me close to him in an attempt to comfort us both.

My brand new husband was sitting in the seat across the aisle from us, looking somewhat irritable, wishing very much to get on with the journey. This was a return trip for him, as he had already been in Canada for several years, and the courtship

1

and the wedding had taken up too much of his time already. Now he was eager to return to his job at the plant. I was all of 18 years of age, and, for the first time, I was leaving behind my country of birth, my parents, small brothers and sisters, for the first time, not knowing when I would return.

> *I am leaving my home, I am leaving my roots.*
> *Where will I fit in?*
> *Where will I belong?*
> *I am a daughter, but I am leaving my parents,*
> *I am a sister, but I have no more siblings.*
> *I am a niece, without any uncles or aunts,*
> *I am a friend, but my friends aren't coming.*
> *I am a poet, but I have no language.*
> *I want to learn, but I cannot speak.*
> *I am not an Anglophone.*
> *I am not a Canadian.*
> *I lost my culture, I lost my language,*
> *I lost my home, I lost my roots.*
> *I have no place to lay my head.*

It was on this somber day in March that I began the difficult process of transcending my culture. I did not know that this would be the real journey upon which I was about to embark. I thought that I was merely coming to Canada. Like any teenager, I concentrated on being born, not on dying. Yet the dying was there all along. First I only called it leaving home. Much later, I was to call it loneliness, or homesickness, or craziness. But at the beginning it was merely a giving up of something in order to find something better, that something better being my own unknown future, the emphasis being on the something better, not on the giving up.

It had been only yesterday , my last day at home, that I had stood looking out over the weeds and the grass that grew at the back of our old house and to the pond that reflected back to me the thoughts and dreams of a young girl on the threshold of life. The silence and peace of the country village had seemed as always more captivating than the sound of a Viennese symphony. If there were any fears or misgivings to be had about the future, I had not yet been aware of them. If I perceived that there was a lot here that I was leaving behind me, never to recapture it, it was not with any great sense of loss.

My mother channelled all her energy into being a perfect mother, while greatly fearing the larger world that I was about to enter. On my wedding day, she wrote a poem for me, a poem which most likely propped up her doubts about her decision to let me leave. She wrote that parents are the living bows from which their children as living arrows are set forth. Afterwards, she was never quite so willing to shoot any more of her arrows so swiftly and so far. None of her other children, save one, would ever acquire any great distance from her, neither in miles nor in differentiation.

The same poignant poem said that she did not desire for me a life free from pain, a rose garden where there were never any tears to be shed, because tears purified the heart and pain refined the spirit. Pain, the poem said, would bring me closer to God and His loving Mother. The poem also spoke of the mountains I would have to climb, and the storms that I would have to endure. Like many women of her culture, she had great devotion to the Mother of God, and she also knew how to tap into the great poetic heritage of the Flemish.

Looking back now, I think that she just happened to find a verse which could articulate all the things that she could not put into words as I prematurely left the nest. I can only wonder now, myself, at what went on in her heart at the time of losing her eldest daughter and helpmate, when, in the midst of grinding poverty, she still had 12 more children to raise. The finality of that parting moment seems hard to imagine now that the Atlantic has shrunk considerably, and jet planes spew their tired cargo daily from their ramps—now that reunions are more or less taken for granted.

But at the time, the script of the future had not as yet been written. There was no hopefully-scheduled distant reunion to look forward to that could take the finality out of separation. The cost of a journey across the Atlantic could feed my mother's family for an entire year, and the prospect of such a venture would, in her case at least, have to remain a dream for the next decade. In the fatality of that moment, she had nothing to give to me except her own courage, and a few thoughtful verses written on a slip of paper, yet the advice given would prove to be on target. I would shed many bitter tears. I would become enured with pain. The emptiness left in my heart by the loss of home, friends, family, and country of birth would decisively shape my life, its failures and its successes.

My reason for leaving Belgium, other than my new husband, had to do with the economic deprivation of the Flemish region at the time. I had been only dimly aware of the shabbiness of the place of my birth. At the age of 10, I had been on my first train journey. It had taken me through the rich suburbs of Belgium, and I remember being astonished by the unfamiliar perfection of the man-made world of the wealthy. The well-kept lawns and flowers, the beautifully-designed architecture had stood in stark contrast to the appalling ugliness and poverty of the environment that I knew, but which, for lack of comparison, I had not really seen until then. I had only been aware of the mesmerizing loveliness of this piece of unspoilt nature which surrounded the house of my birth now before me.

Until that first encounter with the world beyond, I had not very much cared that we were poor. My mother, having had a too strict upbringing herself, had insisted on giving us the joys and freedoms of an unencumbered childhood. As children, we were allowed to play for hours in reckless abandon. We had the unparalleled freedom of a large family growing up in a country village, secure in our possession of the love and attention of two loving parents. That this love and attention was a reaction to their own deprived childhood would only become apparent much later. Just then, we knew little about the daily worries and anxieties of our parents, of their poverty, or their impoverished relationships with my grandparents.

There were times that we sensed what was going on. Like the time that the man from welfare surveyed the ancient slum dwelling we called our home. My great-grandfather had fixed up the place at the lowest point of Flanders' economic depression at the turn of the 19th century. Built originally from mud and plaster, he had used prewar throwaway material to "renovate" it. The result was a shelter in which any woman could waste the best years of her life in endless tasks of seemingly futile housekeeping and frustrating rounds of cleaning and straightening up. And this was indeed the way my mother's life was eaten up most of the time.

The welfare man had come, dressed in a good suit and tie, and I, a sensitive little girl, winced inwardly for my mother as well as for myself. I well remember the arrogant and scornful eye wandering through every tiny room of our house. I felt ashamed and exposed, in the way that only poor people know. My mother was hoping that the house would be condemned, so that she could apply for assistance for the construction of a better house. Many government programs were under way to build better housing, but the welfare man had been apathetic; "just doing a job," no doubt. The house may have qualified as a condemned building in his own mind, but he was not about to allow any state assistance to flow toward this poor province of Flanders. If people were lazy and stupid, that was their problem, not his.

At this time, in that part of my native land, economic development had not spread either its blessings or its curses. My father had a small business but it paid little. Sometimes his earnings of one day could be spent on a magazine subscription. Money was always scarce. When there was no money, it was up to me or my eldest brother to go to the store and charge everything. The store owners were kind and they knew that eventually payment would be forthcoming. When I left home to emigrate to Canada, my parents had given me the equivalent of $20.00, which was more than they could afford. Never did I want to be poor again!

In my teenage years, I had also begun to understand the harshness of being at the bottom end of society. My first inkling that I was not good enough was communicated to me by my teachers. The nuns had already drilled into me a concept of the Catholic Ideal Thing. Every good Catholic girl was supposed to measure up to this ideal, but few succeeded. Those who measured up, the extremely good and beautiful, were allowed to be the Virgin Mary in the school play. Tied up mysteriously with Catholic perfection was the social esteem that could be had only if one had proper clothes to wear and a decent home.

Centuries after the French Revolution, vestiges of class-consciousness still remained deeply buried in European society. The social snobbery toward working people was matched only by the snobbery of the working class toward the rich. In addition, World War II had left in its wake a hatred toward those who had been accused of collaborating with the Germans during the war. My mother's family had been thus falsely accused, and my father, by sticking up for my mother, had managed to get himself jailed at the time that I was born. People in small villages have long memories, and the stigma attached to our family did nothing to improve our social confidence.

In those long bygone years, there were many parents who went without the bare necessities in order to ensure somehow that at least one of their boys would get higher education. Those who could afford higher education saw it as a sure means of escaping the narrow confines of the village mentality. If one could manage somehow to have one's children belong to the local club of university students, one hoped at least that they would be safe from all social contempt. Brothers and sisters were expected to assist in carrying the financial burden of sending the chosen ones away to a university. It was not until many years later, when I had a chance to continue my education at a Canadian university, that I realized how deeply embedded class distinctions had been in the consciousness of my family of origin. The reaction of some of my relatives to my university education was to alternate between pride, scorn, and noncomprehending envy. In the process of transcending my background and culture, I would obviously go too far.

I also became aware at an early age of the bleak reality facing those who had been born female. A higher education for a poor girl was never even considered. The boys needed their schooling so that they could make a decent living. But education was very expensive, and for a girl it was thought of as money wasted. I had a natural and insatiable curiosity combined with a quick and easy intelligence that would have taken me far into the world of academic pursuit. It was not to be, however. The road for me was already mapped out around the triple confinement of kitchen, church and children. The first two did not appear to be such frightening prospects, but any thought of the latter filled me with a despair which I was at a loss to define.

It had always seemed to me as if every poor woman in the village was pregnant all the time, and my earliest perception of pregnancy did not hold any promise of the wealth of motherhood, but rather the threat of the endless trap of poverty. To be a girl and a woman meant that biology was destiny. Life was something beyond a woman's control, something that happened to her, not something in which she had any say. My female body had the power to control me, to control who I would be and what I would do, or better, what I would not be and what I would not be able to do.

It was not that I did not like children. I was crazy in love with my little brothers and sisters, and not to be able to see them growing up would become a persistent void in my future life. Until my marriage at the age of 18, however, I had identified completely with my mother, and I had been thrust into the mothering role long before I had a chance to develop my own identity. The result was that I was now anxious to find my own identity in life, and that included not getting pregnant too soon. My mother however, for reasons of her own, did not believe in birth control, and my future years were to be plagued with countless nightmares in which I dreamt that my mother was pregnant again, as she was pregnant now, at the time of my leaving.

The trip to Canada by cargo ship lasted 10 days. At first I sat on deck a lot, looking at the ship's stern rising high before my eyes every time a giant wave lifted it into the air. When my stomach began to heave and toss in rhythmic unison with the struggling vessel, my new husband was annoyed with my seasickness, and I moved to my cabin below deck.

After a few days, I began to feel better. The ship was meant for cargo, but it did have some passengers, all of them travelling first class. The boat that we were supposed to travel on had been unable to navigate, with the result that we now found ourselves on this ship in the company of these well-to-do passengers. I felt out of place and ill at ease. I did not know how to dress for dinner, or how to converse in English with my dinner companions. Even if I had known how much to tip, I did not have enough money for tips. In spite of every drawback, I felt the adventuresomeness of the young. This was the beginning of my new life, and the sweetness of adventure soon overcame any other misgivings that I may have had.

The most difficult part of my new adventure right now was the language. I had begun to study English at home because I loved languages. My mother had been glad of my interest in learning even if she hated the English language. She never learned to like the sound of it. It was completely foreign to her.

Actually, now that I was beginning to feel submerged in an English-speaking culture, I did not much like the sound of it either. I could barely pick up a spoken word here and there. Even though I had enjoyed reading English poetry and doing grammar exercises, now that I was suddenly transported into a scene where people carried on what seemed to me the non-comprehensible jargon of birds twittering, I spent so much energy concentrating on the structure and sound of words and sentences that I often missed out entirely on the messages that these same words and sentences conveyed. I had so much difficulty in understanding that for a long time I remained impervious to human kindness and rudeness alike.

We landed in New York when the melting snow was turning everything into an ugly brown. For some people their first encounter with the Americas gives them a feeling of exuberance and exhilaration which they have difficulty describing. For me this kind of exhilaration would only come later. On that cold day in March, the vastness of space and the feeling of freedom that accompanies it escaped me altogether. The dismal early March landscape left me feeling as if I had just entered the land God gave to Cain.

Chapter Two

A Rough Beginning

"Don't put everything over on my side, you bastard."

The woman working across the assembly line from me hollered over the noise of the meat slicers and sausage skinners. Her fat, ugly face was contorted with rage. Now that my English was improving, my previous lack of comprehension no longer provided a buffer against the rudeness and vileness of the language.

I was slow.

I was also terrified. I was not used to being spoken to in this way.

I had never worked in a factory before. But I was leaving too much work to do for the other women, who were working on the other side of the fast-moving conveyor belt which carried sliced bacon to be wrapped into packages.

I learned to work faster. But it didn't help much. They still treated me like dirt.

When I did too little they were on my back. But when I began to do more they criticized me too. "You want to do everything around here?" one woman sneered. It was a no-win situation. They had it in for me and they rejected any attempts on my part to become their friend.

I went home every night dreading the next day. And every Sunday afternoon, I suffered anxiety attacks thinking that tomorrow I would have to start another week.

My first task had been to find work. That's how I had landed
this job in a meat-packing plant, the same place where my husband had worked before. I had been thrilled at the thought that
I was going to be making money for the first time in my life.
But the work in this place had seemed unbelievably demanding,
and the white smocks that they gave me to cover up my clothes
seemed more demeaning than any of the hand-me-downs that I
had ever had to wear as a child. And no one, but no one, had
warned me about the speed of the assembly line, about the
coarse and vulgar language of the workers, or about their
meanness to newcomers in the workplace.

After the first weeks, I began to buckle under the stress of
the crude verbal attacks of the women and, since I was young
and pretty, the sexual harassment of the men. Many a weekend
I spend being physically ill at the thought of having to spend
another day in that place. But there was no one to talk to, no
home to return to, no parents to shelter me now. I projected my
need for a father figure on the foreman, a big man with a round
face, blue eyes, and a receding hairline, who always looked as if
he was personally responsible for every move that was made.
He would stand beside me with a stopwatch, timing the number
of items that I could move in a minute.

When I got to know him better, I discovered that he had
neither a great sense of responsibility nor concern for anyone.
The only motive that kept any or all of the foremen going was
fear. Fear of losing their favored position if there was any slack-
ening of production on the line.

Strangely enough, after some time, I learned to like the work
at the assembly line. Its speed was challenging, and the only
thing that kept the work from becoming soul-destroying monot-
ony. I also learned to speak the language, and much of its vocabulary of obscene words would continue to serve me as an
inward safety valve, their hidden power effective even in the
most solemn of occasions.

The cruelty of my coworkers to newcomers, especially to
those who could not speak the language, taught me much about
human nature, and its curious mixture of good and evil. There
was one assistant foreman whose name was Louie. He had

come from Hungary and his English was pretty good. His presence there made a great difference for me. It is difficult to describe him, other than that he looked Hungarian. He had the joyful courage in the face of adversity of many of the people of his homeland. Unlike my own people who had lacked the confidence of a strong national identity, his people had communicated to him that wherever he went he could be proud of his origins. Proud too, of the fact that he was a "blue-collar working man." He could use foul language with the worst of them, but he never lost his dignity. It was his pride and confidence that shone through in his actions. I was glad of his presence and took heart from it.

There was also Carol. She was barely 20, a couple of years older than myself. She had chestnut hair, arched eyebrows and a delicate nose. Her brown eyes reflected every nuance of her volatile temperament. When she was cheerful, she made everyone else feel cheerful, but when she was angry she let everyone know too. As a result the foreman sometimes tried to appease her by assigning to her an easier job.

And I learned fast.

Next time I was sent upstairs to help with the butchering of hogs, I came down and let everyone know by the look on my face that I had been mortally offended by having been forced to do work that I considered to be beneath my dignity. The foreman quickly tried to appease me by letting me do something nice for the rest of the day.

Carol had a quality of honesty about her which I had never before experienced in my neat and pious life of disciplinary restrictions and inhibitions. She also had spunk and endurance, qualities that I was only just beginning to discover in myself.

But she also had the self-destructive traits of those who are too bright and too gifted for the meager opportunities afforded them. Often, when she came to work in the morning, she boastfully and accurately could tell how many ounces of gin she had in the course of a weekend, but more often than not she couldn't remember the names of the men who had taken her to bed.

Because of people such as these, I discovered the warmth of those who live by their gut feelings, but also that peculiar envy and hostility of those who despise their way of life. I learned that if the workers hated everyone who was courteous and polite, it was because courtesy and good manners stood for everything that was unattainable to them. Working endless hours in a monotonous routine work which left their spirits sapped and their brains numb, the niceties of life took on an obscene quality. They hated the circumstances of their life which forced them into endless hours of exploitative labor with no hope of moving out.

They especially hated immigrants who still had hope, hope of finding a better life. For an immigrant like myself, this work was only a stepping-stone to the better life that I had come to Canada to seek. Too many of these people had forgotten how to hope. Consequently, they were caught in endless rounds of making and spending money. It was the only way they knew to survive.

Fresh from the mystical symbiosis with family and earth, I soaked up the influences of these people, and their various personalities. I learned to speak their language and to call things by their real names. These men and women may have despised their own lack of veneer, but the values that they did possess had nothing to do with the veneer of civilized living or the shallow kindness of those who lived by their brains and not by their guts. Tough, street-smart, and in touch with the rawest of emotions, they taught me lessons that would last me a lifetime. I was to remember this time of my life with gratitude; it had given me an inside view of life in the pits.

Two days before Christmas, Carol and Louie each brought me a small gift. Their words were few, but their smiling faces spoke volumes. I had won my first battle. I was loved, I was accepted, I was happy.

Shortly after, the company went bankrupt, proof perhaps that shortchanging the workers is no guarantee to the viability of the company. Up to this day, it still gives me a momentary glimpse of triumph when I take the car for a spin over the parking lot where once upon a time bulldozers, without pomp or ceremony, buried the old vestiges of Brown Packing Co.

The difference between the two worlds that I encountered that first year was indicative of many of the choices that I would make in later life. I would never lose that painful awareness of the split between the world of the nice and pious people of the church community which I had joined, and that other world of those whose dreary lives were made bearable only with too much booze and too much sex. People whose instant hate and mistrust toward me had eventually eased into a grudging acceptance. The contrast between the two worlds provided me with a perspective which would help shape and mold my mature values.

Chapter Three
More Pain Than Wisdom

I cleaned away the dirty dishes, and piled them beside the sink. The good meal that I had prepared had soon disappeared, the men had gone on some urgent errand, and here I was cleaning up. After that, there were loads of wash to do, and the bread to bake.

I could see my elderly neighbor walking over to the back door, her arms filled with tender stalks of rhubarb from the garden.

"Maybe you can use some of these to make jam," she said.

I knew that she was a little suspicious of all these men who were living with me in the tiny apartment, so I decided to put her mind at ease.

"Those guys are Daniel's brothers," I said.

She wasn't convinced, but she was nice just the same.

If only she knew how short-lived my happy honeymoon had been. By midsummer, after only four months in Canada, I had changed from the role of mother to my little brothers and sisters to the role of caretaker of a series of in-laws. When I had been coparenting my siblings, I still had my mother there to make sure that my own needs were not forgotten. My new role of caretaker to those who also wanted to explore the opportunities of this country was different. As the elder brother's wife, I was needed to give comfort and sympathy in the shape of unlimited hospitality, free meals and clean clothes, but my own emotional space decreased as the number of opportunity seekers grew.

While I seemed to have salvaged nothing of my past life, my husband now found in the brothers who came to join him the family that he had missed in his first two solitary years in Canada. With a new wife, and a succession of adventuresome brothers, he now felt more complete and happy than ever before. Brimming with ambition, and bursting with the hope for the good life that only an immigrant knows, his only dream was to be a big farmer. As for every true farmer, farming was the only thing he knew about; it was the only thing he cared for, the sole subject of all his conversations, in short, his only reason for living. That, and the family clan which was now, partially at least, on the same side of the ocean. In their youthful arrogance, and at the peak of their chauvinism, they were too caught up in their own world to concern themselves with "women's feelings."

For the three first months of our marriage, our little apartment had provided us with the privacy which would become such a scarce commodity in the years that followed. We had some time at least in which to discover the joys of married life. The nightmares of the job faded into oblivion when on the weekend we had slept late and made love repeatedly. Now we had people living with us, so I concentrated on creating a sense of family right there which included all of them, and this family that I was creating was somewhat of a substitute for the family that I had lost. But how could I explain to them that I had once had a family, too, and that I missed them daily? So I began at a very early age to experience how oblivious happy people are to the unhappiness of others.

Daniel and his three brothers took it for granted that I would make their first Christmas away from home a happy one, and I willingly obliged. Hadn't I always done this? That first Christmas, at least, I managed to forget my own loneliness. The small presents from Carol and Louie had given me a reason to be happy, and my first Christmas dinner had turned out well.

That evening, in the apartment upstairs from us, children were playing noisily. And for one magic moment they had be-

come, in my mind's eye, the happy noises of my little brothers
and sisters playing. Tomorrow might bring more than its share
of sorrow, but today I was content.

On Valentine's Day we celebrated our first wedding anniver-
sary by purchasing a farm, a place of our own. All that winter I
had gone farm hunting together with my husband and two of
his brothers. There were dozens of farms for sale in the area
that year, all of them cheap. All we needed was to find someone
who would be willing to keep the mortgage. The banks had
turned down our request for a loan, and so had the Farm Credit
Corporation. Serious money lenders could not see how we would
be able to operate a dairy farm with the little savings that we
had. They were right, of course. We had put away every penny
that we made at our jobs, and we had only enough for a small
down payment on a farm.

After looking at dozens of farms and trying to negotiate
terms with just as many sellers, we found a farmer who had
recently lost his only son, and who was willing to give a young
man a chance. He was not overly concerned about making
money out of the sale of his farm, but instead he wanted us to
have his place for a reasonable down payment. He would also
hold the mortgage at the regular rate of interest. The day we
signed the agreement was exactly one year after our wedding
day.

Then it was time to begin scouting farm sales for used farm
equipment. The brothers pooled all their resources that spring
to buy an old tractor, a plow, a disc, and a cultivator to work
our land. We also bought our first 12 Holstein cows which officially started us in the dairy business.

I had never been a farmer before, and I learned something
new every day. I now had a place to call home, but I was poorer
than I had ever been. The little money that we had was all used
up, and the bills for seed, fertilizer and feed started to come. I
had never been very good at tolerating debt, and I secretly
longed for a safe and secure place where I would be free of debt,
with $20 stuffed in an old stocking somewhere for security's
sake. But my life was not to be a secure one. For the next 25

years I would be doing cash flows and juggling bills, and as the farm grew so did the amount of money borrowed. I did grow more tolerant to the ins and outs of the business world, although I cannot say that I ever came to like it. I always hated to be in debt.

I found that I preferred farm work to factory work. For many years to come I hated to live what seemed to be so far out in the country. I was used to having people all around, and here the neighbors were sparse and distant. However, I savored the closeness to nature and the unforced style of farm living. Occasionally, I also enjoyed long informal chats with the men who helped us work the land, the veterinarians, or the neighbors

After some of my in-laws went back to Belgium to live, I no longer had to keep house for them, but now I was cooking for the men who helped with the haying, harvesting, silo-filling, or tilling. I could never figure out why farm women took it for granted that it was their job to "feed the men." I had never met any man who was willing to make it his career to "feed the women." And if I was not feeding men in the house, I was chasing down Daniel in some distant field to bring him lunch. The guys must have thought that this was what I was put on earth for. When anyone asked me "what do you do?" my answer was unerringly, "nothing."

Living on the farm, I was lonelier than I had ever been. It is difficult to describe the kind of loneliness that an immigrant experiences when cut off from all previous ties. Most of the time, I was not even aware of it, I was too busy helping out. But then some day, the doorbell would ring, or a car seemed to slow down as if it was about to stop at the house, and my heart started pounding and my hands began too shake; and I would once again feel that much-too-frequent desperate surge of longing, a yearning to see a dear, familiar face again. This intolerable longing was always followed by the bleak realization that I was trapped. I could not afford to travel at will to see my loved ones once again.

This intense physical and emotional reaction which overcame me time and again continued until it started to drive me crazy. It hindered me from making friends in my new environment.

Every encounter with any human being would for the longest time remain only second best, because no one could ever fill the hole in my heart that had been left by the loss of my loved ones. It was not until after many years, when I became secure in my knowledge that I could choose to travel back and forth to Belgium whenever I would feel the need for it, that my anxiety began to subside.

The only old and familiar face that I saw, that first year, was my mother-in-law. A Flemish group of people had created an association named Vlakanam, a name so chosen because it designated that all its members had one thing in common, they all had relatives in Canada or the U.S. Members of this association could then charter a group flight at greatly reduced rates. Charter flights were to become a blessing for those who could little afford the journey across the ocean, yet who very much wanted to visit a son, a daughter, or any other relative. My mother-in-law was among those first adventuresome relatives who crossed the ocean by chartered plane. That first trip, she and the rest of the group endured the discomfort of a demanding twenty-four-hour voyage with many stops and transfers; but by so doing she opened up a way for us to keep in touch with our people back home.

Because of the expense and difficulty involved, her stays were often lengthy. My mother-in-law stayed for six weeks. Her visit turned out to be very rewarding for my husband and his brothers, but bitterly disappointing for me. Observing their happy togetherness made it even more difficult for me to deny my own emotional needs. In fact, it was the beginning of a new kind of emotional torture for me. It was my own parents whom I wanted, my own brothers and sisters, my own friends.

Most immigrants are familiar with this unique kind of conflict. Their longing is for their own folks. Consequently, they often lavish unlimited hospitality on any guest who even vaguely reminds them of their homeland, anyone who comes to visit or just to explore the country, a relation of a relation, a friend of a friend, just anyone. Any mention of a possible visitor had me all tied up in knots, my emotions a tangle of longing and fear, of need and apprehension, of desperation and loneliness. But after bestowing too much hospitality on the visitor, I often felt like a doormat. I was depleted from weeks of playing hostess and chief entertainer, but what I really longed for had not been fulfilled. I had not been able to reclaim that part of myself that I had lost through the severing of my ties with my own people. The old adage, that those who give out of their need are doubly blessed, somehow did not cut it. I was giving out of my need, and I did not feel blessed at all.

These encounters were not entirely without benefit, however. Through these experiences I discovered that the key to my own selfhood lay not only in these relationships, but in my own goals, aspirations and successes, whichever way I would define them. But how difficult it was to set up any goals and aspirations without money, without any knowledge of the world in which I now lived, and how impossible it was to aspire to one's own aims when one's role is already defined by the rules of the society in which one lives. To be a helpmate, to be a comforter, to be a housekeeper, to be for others but never for oneself.

As long as I still had a sense of connection with my country of birth, as long as I still felt the love of my parents, heard their voices in the corners of my mind, as long as I perceived that I had their blessing, I had felt strong and full of adventure. As time went on, I lost all contact and even all memory of that early symbiosis with my family and my country of origin. Those memories that remained became a painful, empty blur. I could no longer bear to look at any of the pictures that connected me with my past. Lives which had been so intertwined with mine were going on without me. My parents had accepted life without me.

It is said that grass grows where no one walks. My memories of my family of origin and my country of birth congealed in the shape that they had been in my eighteenth year. Meantime, the mere mention of my remote and invisible family to the people in my new world produced glassy stares, bored indifference or simple annoyance at my sentimental attachments to a country the existence of which they could not even fathom. I felt like a widow, who, realizing that she is annoying everyone by talking about her dead husband, wisely avoids talking about him at all. The worst part was that once you have lost your family and friends, people soon forget that you ever had anyone to love and care about, that you ever had anyone who loved and cared about you. I found some comfort with people who through sheer old age had lost everyone dear to them, and who had nothing but their dignity and pride to cling to, but I also grew ashamed of my attachment to my parents, my brothers and sisters, the country of my birth. I began to see it as something ugly, something no one wanted to hear about, a sign of weakness on my part.

I knew that by leaving my culture I had been made different, distinct from my people in Belgium, but also from the people here who had a sense of belonging to the local town, the local church, and the local culture with its well-defined rules. I just did not know, as yet, how to value that difference. At times, I felt the contrary pull of my strong spirit of adventure and the need to come to appreciate this being different. But I dreaded the challenge that lay before me. I was conscious only of a fervent and painful longing to regain the sense of belonging that I had enjoyed before I had come to Canada, and the more I realized that this was impossible, the more I clung to this longing.

In time, the challenge that my own life represented would take a clearer shape in my mind, but for now it was too vague and too confusing, a mystery still to be explored. I had adopted a new land and a new culture, and by so doing I had transcended the makings of any culture, never to belong wholly and unquestionably to any culture ever again. I was never again to possess that unconscious kind of belonging, that feeling of being part of it all, that people have who remain within the boundaries of their home and culture.

In losing my connection with my country of birth and my family of origin, however, I felt as if I had lost my main source of strength. I no longer wanted to search for my place in life, for my own uniqueness. Many years later, when finally I would be in a position to put my own life into perspective, I would come to understand that the prolonged depression, which came to be my constant companion in life, had started then already. The normal and healthy depression that human beings suffer in the process of giving up the familiar in life in order to move into an unknown future can easily turn into a chronic, pathological depression if certain "things" had been taken away from a young person long before he or she is psychologically ready to give them up. Like many girls who had married at 18 and left behind all that they had known before, I was not strong enough to accept what seemed at the time to be the final and irreversible loss of my loved ones and my beloved country, and this loss would intermittently tear me apart with disabling distortion.

* * *

Meanwhile, as potential friends, my in-laws had proved to be a mixed blessing. The first person with whom I had become friends while in this country had been my one brother-in-law, Gilbert. He lived with us and helped us with everything. He rewired the barn, and in spite of his degree in engineering, he helped with cleaning out stables, unloading hay, moving harvested grain, and remodelling the barn. Somehow his friendship, which was to last for only two years, made up for the constant interference, the lack of privacy, and the emotional demands that only parents of teenagers know, but that I came to experience too soon because my in-laws had no other place but mine that they could call home. After two years, however, Gilbert went back to Belgium to pursue the life for which he had trained. I had grown fond of him and I missed him terribly. He, soon got caught up in his new career in Belgium, and little did he remember the woman who had been like a sister to him while he was in Canada.

Shortly after he left, however, a younger brother arrived, Andy, who came full of innocent excitement and childlike adventuresomeness.

Unknown to any of us, Andy had a latent schizophrenia which would cause great trauma in our own lives, a trauma which would leave me devastated. For the one year that Andy was here, our lives, which were already riddled by debt and worry, would take on a roller coaster quality caused by emotional involvement with an illness that we did not understand nor know how to cope with.

Having lost my own ties, I protectively reached out to this young man who was Daniel's youngest brother. At first, I tried to make his adjustment period in his new country as painless as possible. Every weekend he came "home" from the place

where he worked and I scheduled nice dinners, interesting out-
ings, and good times to make him feel at home. When, after
only a few months, he grew tired of his work, he talked us into
going to Belgium for Christmas and he offered to look after the
farm for us. Needless to say, Daniel and I did not need too
much coaxing on that account. I could not pass up such an offer
for me to go to visit my folks after four years of absence.

That very first time we went to Belgium, we had a wonderful
time and we came back more homesick than ever. We had to
give up everything all over again. Unfortunately, at this time
Andy decided to quit his job, and make his home with us on a
permanent basis. Not only did he think of Daniel as the Dad
that he never had, he also thought of our farm as his project
and he wanted a chance to run our place as if it was his own. In
short, he acted as if he was our teenage son. Shortly thereafter,
he showed the first symptoms of schizophrenia.

While in Belgium, I had received long letters from Andy
which made me very uncomfortable indeed, so when the first
symptoms of schizophrenia struck I already knew that something was wrong. However, we felt indebted to him. Had he not
given us the our first chance to visit our homeland?

It took from January to June to sort everything out. What
became increasingly clear was that by moving in with us, Andy
had become too demanding. He also reluctantly, and for a time,
at least, agreed to take medication. In the end, he also decided
that he was not cut out for the harsh life of an immigrant, and
he decided to go back to Belgium. We, on our part, realized that
we had been trying to fill a void in our own life by becoming
overly involved with Daniel's brothers. That's when we decided
it was time to put in an application for the adoption of a child of
our own.

Unfortunately, however, this incident had some bad reverberations in the home of my in-laws. My mother-in-law, needing a
scapegoat, too easily believed that I was to blame for Andy's
problems. I have since discovered that to this day, too often relatives are still blamed for the illness of a schizophrenic. The
stresses that Andy experienced no doubt aggravated his latent
predisposition to the disease, but I had not brought it on.

Once back with his family at home, and removed from the demands and responsibilities of his job in his new country, my brother-in-law enjoyed a temporary reprieve from the effects of his illness. It was several years before his symptoms became so bad again that he had to be treated. Until then my in-laws, as a family, were convinced that I had prefabricated the story of Andy's schizophrenia in order to be rid of him. After that incident, I refused to take on any more boarders, in-laws or not.

I was hurt. I felt that I cared for Andy as I would have cared for a child of my own. I had spent many nights sitting up with him, comforting, trying to talk sense into him. Only a parent of a schizophrenic teenager knows how debilitating such a job can be. I was sure that I would lose my sanity myself. However, I could not defend myself; I had no way to communicate with them. When, years later, they realized that they had made a mistake, that I had diagnosed Andy's situation correctly, I had suffered from their incrimination for so long that I no longer cared about their apologies.

As it so often happens, I felt betrayed by the fact that my husband's strongest loyalty seemed to be on the side of his mother and siblings. As was to be a pattern for both of us, the absence of our relatives left us with so much unfinished business that it would often seem as if our primary loyalties remained with our families of origin. It was fortunate for both of us that we could understand this need in each other. Nevertheless, our persistent need for connection with our distant families of origin never quite lost its threatening power. This insight, too, sheds its own light on the life of the immigrant. No one would suspect that the lonely immigrant has his or her "interfering" relatives, also. The fact is, however, that great distances between family members cause their own kind of interference in the normal processes of family interaction, and this may obstruct the family's adaptability and stunt the healthy growth of its individual members.

Yet this incident taught us in some small way to protect our marriage from undue demands and interference from others, and we were to remember what we had learned until the day came that these overly demanding "others" would be our own teenage children.

We also learned to limit our responsibilities toward others. We learned to separate our own needs from those of others, and not to mix them up in a single batch. Like many immigrant women especially, I had tried to fill the empty spaces in my heart, spaces created by loss of family and home country, by looking after other newcomers to this country. Newcomers, who like all young adults, still needed the comforts and security of a home away from home, yet who did not feel obliged to return any loyalty or gratitude toward the people who offered them unlimited hospitality. On the contrary, in the way of teenagers they often resented their rather unusual situation of dependency. This, too, taught me a lot about being a parent to young adults.

Like all young people, Daniel's brothers had still needed a place that they could call home, but they also wanted to know and feel that they were individuals who could stand on their own feet. Because they were away from their homeland and their friends, however, they had to accomplish their independence without the usual confidence that familiar surroundings, as well as their peers, could have given them. This only increased their dependence on me; but it was a dependence that they did not want.

It was my 21st birthday when we took Andy to the airport. I cried for a week and then I cut off my long blond hair. I had tried to be a saint the way I had been brought up to be. Self-effacing, self-sacrificing, loving others, never being for myself, and I had failed.

In retrospect, I see now how these bad experiences with my in-laws were the beginning of a turning point in my life. I was forced to question much of what I had perceived my role in life to be. I had come to Canada in search of my own identity. Instead I had found myself pushed deeper into the demands of a woman's role and a woman's place, and for the first time I had experienced the terror of losing myself into that role. Too slowly I would begin to awaken to the realization that I would have to learn to be for myself before I could also be for others.

The path to sainthood goes through adulthood. . .
Ego boundaries must be hardened before they can be
softened. An identity must be established before it can
be transcended. One must find one's self before one
can lose it.[1]

At the age of 21, I had already been faced with as many responsibilities and decisions as many people twice my age are faced with. Furthermore, I had to make these decisions without the confidence of my own independent insights, and without the warmth and living skills of others who could have helped me through such trying times.

After this grueling episode, my fears of the complexity and confusion of life proved so great that I shut down any emotions I may have felt. To protect myself against any more unbearable hurt, I drew up a new map of reality by which I could love people without getting close to them, or without being emotionally involved with them.

I became the iron-willed little scrapper. As long as my own goals seemed impossible to achieve, as long as relationships never worked out, there was nothing else for me to do than to settle for other people's goals instead. I shovelled feed, I cleaned out calf pens, stood around for hours helping my husband in the freezing cold, handing him tools and encouragement. I grew increasingly disappointed with the poor returns for all my efforts. When people began to compliment us on how successful we were in our farm operation, I did not feel successful, because I was not a success in my own eyes. I gave up hope because I did not even know what, if anything, I was hoping for. Like the dog in the hot-wired cage, I no longer knew which way to move in order to avoid the pain of electric shock. I wanted to huddle in misery, not knowing what to do.

Chapter Four

Breaking Out of the Mold

My husband and I timidly sat down on a dark brown wooden bench outside in the tiny hallway, and we waited. Daniel felt mortified. I was dead set on adopting a child and I had dragged him here to the Children's Aid Society. A young man crossed the hall, glancing at us indifferently as he passed by us.

"What's with them, are they lost or something?" we heard him say to the girl inside. They acted as if we were not there.

Daniel whispered, "We don't have to do this; we could still wait until we have children of our own," he said, desperately.

"Everything will work out fine, you'll see," I reassured him.

But when I had gone to see my obstetrician, he had told me in no uncertain terms that "it cost money to battle infertility." He did not even consider that the infertility problem might lay with Daniel. And I was much too eager to take all the responsibility in order to protect my husband's male ego.

Eventually someone took notice of us. "You are in the wrong place," the girl said. "You must go to your local C.A.S."

That day we officially began the process of the adoption of our baby girl.

After four years of marriage we had remained childless. It was not so much because I was unhappy that we had no children, I still had many ambivalent feelings about whether or not I even wanted to produce my own children. In the culture of the time, it was taken for granted that this was what a couple wanted. One did not have too much choice in the matter.

Moreover, I belonged to a Church which had never allowed much freedom in the way of personal feelings and individual choice in regards to birth control and fecundity, so I could find no help there. Even if I did not want to join the multitudes who grew indifferent to what the Church said and thought in regard to birth control, neither could I join those who unquestioningly accepted Catholic values as their personal values.

However, I did not want to go the way of my mother so that my life would be determined by my biology. I wanted to have some control over my life; I needed so badly to know that I had some choice in my life right now. Adopting a child gave me that choice toward my own life and destiny.

It also seemed to me, at the time, a unique way to extend myself, and it made me feel in a position of strength. To have become pregnant would have thrown me back into a position of weakness and helplessness, or so I thought.

How could I be having a baby, in a hospital with no one there to come and visit me, no grandparents to make me feel that continuation of love and mutual joy that only a family can provide?

Daniel had only me on whom he could depend. The ancient farm equipment plus the endless hours of hard manual labor did not allow for too much more sickness or disability on my part. My health was already iffy at best with premenstrual or postmenstrual pains, and everything in between. I was already beginning to believe those who claim that biology is destiny were right. To live in a body that fails more often than not does not leave too much room for freedom of action, feminine pad commercials notwithstanding.

And then there was the slight little matter of my emotional numbness. I doubted very much that I would make a very enthusiastic mother. Having a baby could only bring me face-to-face with the abandoned child in myself. The abandoned child was there, not by reason of my having been abandoned as a child, but because all my childhood connections and memories had been lost in my struggle to adapt to my new homeland. And so, I lived with my secret ambivalence. There was no one to whom I could talk, other than Daniel, and he was as confused and scared as I was.

I would probably have felt less ambivalent if it had not been for my own theological bent.

The material poverty of my background had been a perfect breeding ground for religious values. There were no T.V. commercials to brainwash us, no shopping centers to distract us, no expensive gadgets to occupy us, no frivolous social life to trick us into an endless cycle of desire and gratification.

I received my Catholic education in the same arid and stultifying way of many in my generation, but somewhere among the orthodox formulas, the legalistic expectations, and the threats of everlasting hell I had still managed to discern the dross from the slag.

The sisters who taught me had been stunted women who had taken a shortcut to holiness by giving up everything long before they had anything to be given up. Mother Superior, who taught me through three grades, spoke of selflessness and self-sacrifice, while her lack of a strong and secure ego often caused her to display bouts of petty envy equal to that of small children. Unknowingly, I fuelled her piously-concealed resentment with my childlike freedom, with the result that I was the recipient of some baffling psychological cruelty.

Much later I realized that the social and religious repression of that time may have stifled their spiritual growth and personal maturity, but it did not have the power to destroy their intimacy with God. Little did I know that my own history would evolve in reaction to that. These women had given up a chance to experience the challenges and dangers of personal freedom for the sake of their faith. Even if I marvelled at these women who had remained cheerfully faithful to their call at the expense of their own personhood, I vowed never to do the same.

Besides from my mother, I also caught my faith from my aunt, my priest friend, and my books. Always fascinated by words, I had read everything in print since I was nine, and I soon knew more about religion, politics and sex than my father. I often had the feeling that my father was the child and I was the adult. Both my friend the priest and my father used to warn me not to read about things that were too complicated for me, but like the children of today I had an insatiable curiosity about life.

I also had a poetic soul. When I read a fine piece of poetry, I would be transported for hours into a mystical world of cosmic dimensions. I could not talk to anyone about this perceptive and sensitive part of my self, so I would sit, in the middle of the day, in the empty village church which smelled of must and scoured flagstones, and in the peaceful stillness I would listen to God and God would listen to me.

My love for poetry, like the love for my parents and my country, would prove to be no asset in the alien and harsh climate of my adult years in Canada, but those sneaky little chats with God any time during the day would become the source of the inner strength and confidence with which I would surprise even myself.

Like my books, my unmarried aunt had also been a great nurturer of my early faith. She had polio when she was a child, and was confined to a wheelchair. I often spent the night at her place because she had no phone and her elderly father was an Alzheimer's patient. In the morning, I wheeled her over to the church for Mass, which she attended daily.

She was a charismatic person, had loads of priests among her friends, and, in spite of my tender age, she confided in me as in an equal. Her love and concern for others made her especially vulnerable as a woman. The same people who came to her for comfort, sympathy, and moral support did very little to give her the appreciation and recognition that her dedicated life as a Christian deserved. Her life and her holiness were to remain hidden except to those who knew her intimately. She may not have had any children of her own, but her life was as full and exemplary as any woman's life.

I also found a good friend in the pastor of the village church. A slight but gentle man, with pensive inward-looking eyes he represented the timeless wisdom of all Flemish poets and lovers. I often had the privilege of sitting in his quiet study where, puffing on his pipe, he always had time to listen attentively to the idealistic dreams and hopes of a young girl. He had been ready for Vatican II years before it took place. He chose lay readers to read from Scripture in the native language during Mass. He also put increased emphasis on Holy Communion, and he turned Easter Week into a parish celebration.

However, just as before the Council the liturgical changes had filled him with new enthusiasm, the confusion caused by the seeming lack of direction in the church, the dissipation of legalistic threats of hell, and the many people leaving religious vocations for the sake of greater freedom for which they were ill prepared seemed to leave him rudderless. Always of feeble health, toward the end of his life his vitality ebbed away, and his priestly life became to him but a painful and bewildering memory.

Undoubtedly, he had been instrumental in giving me a new Church, but it was a Church in which he no longer felt at home. The Catholic culture was changing, but the best part of his life had been lived in the old culture. The new culture remained for him a source of puzzlement and anguish. In that he was only one of the many innovators of Vatican II who had been carried by the love for their people and the love of their Church to change the liturgical celebrations in the Church, so that they would recapture anew the essence of the Christian faith. Like so many others, he had not been able to foresee the immense suffering that would have to be endured by those who wished to remain faithful to a vision of a renewed and a more human Church. It would be left to my generation to discover that the birth of this Church was also a death, and that the hard and bitter agony of this birth would last many a decade.

That the dying and rebirth of that church would become intertwined with my own process of death and birth was still before me to discover. And as part of this new culture, I too would have to suffer the rift which emerged between those who had undertaken the arduous journey into new territory, and those who clutched desperately to the old gods.

From my friendship with the priest, I learned that I was valuable as a person. He taught me never to cling to anything that could rob me of inner freedom and to entrust all my needs to the Lord. From my friendship with my aunt, I learned the true joy of having a prayerful relationship with God. I also learned that such a relationship was no guarantee against suffering and pain.

The year of my 21st birthday, the same year that my in-laws had given me so much trouble, and only three years after I had left my homeland for good, the first inkling of my theological giftedness and insightfulness had already become a source of frustration and a cause for hostility, ridicule and fear.

I had received a letter from an editor of a Catholic periodical on Christian Marriage. Swept away by the first post-conciliar enthusiasm, such magazines were the beginning of grass-root theological renewal in Belgium. In the letter this priest and theologian asked me to share my writing and my insights with the reading public. I never answered the letter for a number of what seemed to me to be good reasons.

The main reason was that Daniel did not share this part of myself, and, as was to become a pattern in our future life, he was often violently opposed to any attempt that I made to pursue an education, especially a theological one.

And I still had not learned to take responsibility for my own life and future.

Moreover, I was seven years younger than my husband. That meant that our relationship had taken on the qualities of a mentor and his protegée. He had come to Canada before me, he could speak the language, he knew something about the culture, and he also was a good farmer, so he had to teach me everything that I knew. Therefore, marriage to Daniel came to mean that he was mentor and protector. When the day would finally come that he felt that he was no longer needed as my protector and mentor, it was to cause a real crisis in our marriage.

For now, however, this crisis still lay far into the future. Presently, it was not lack of love and caring that kept me imprisoned, but too much closeness and mutual need. Like many couples who suffer from too much closeness and too much togetherness, any sign of differentiation on my part was a threat to my husband's world, a world not of deep layers of critical thought, but one of bricks and stones.

In this world of interminable farm chores, where the role of a woman was defined most narrowly as "helpmate," and in this Church where few voices had begun to question the dehumanizing reduction of women to only parts of themselves, i.e., those parts that have to do with the dispensing of comfort, of mother love, of home care and moral values, there simply was no space for any budding giftedness which did not fit the stereotype.

Life had to be lived and decisions had to be made, however. All I knew then was that I was determined to live my own life, somehow, within the confines of the society in which I lived. Adoption gave me the chance to have children when and if I wanted them. Other people may have seen our decision to adopt a child as a failure on my part, the failure to become pregnant and have a child of my own, but for me it was a chance to express who I was. Much later, as time went on, I, too, would begin to feel as if I had somehow failed the basic test of womanhood, but at this young age there was no sign yet of a biological clock urgently ticking the time away.

Mary Elisabeth came into our lives, shortly after her first birthday, wearing a pink dress and little white shoes. I had not given a child its bath since I had left my parent's home more than four years earlier, but I still knew how to change diapers, bathe the baby, and play hide and seek with her around the house. So much did Daniel and I enjoy our newfound parenthood that it wasn't long before we adopted Timmy, a nine-month-old little boy, an event which made Mary Elisabeth very happy. For awhile, our family consisted of mother, father, a daughter and a son, and we felt complete. It was not until Tim was 10 and Mary Elisabeth was 12 that we expanded on this perfect group by adopting a handsome six-year-old boy who tacitly became the apple of my eye.

* * *

I was never sure then how our relatives in Belgium would accept our adopted children, and I still desperately wanted their approval. Parents of immigrants had enough trouble accepting the fact that their grandchildren were raised to speak a foreign language, but these children did not only speak a different language, they were of a different nationality. Mary Elisabeth was of Scottish parentage, and Timmy's folks were Greek. I knew how my mother felt about the English language, about foreigners, and about people who by some freak of nature did not produce their own children. Again, distance and lack of communication played havoc with my fears.

I had a recurring dream, in which I was plodding along in the shallow end of the swimming pool and my mother was swimming along in the deep end with strong and confident strokes. My legs hurt and I could barely move them. I felt an overwhelming sense of inferiority to my mother who had mastered the art of swimming so easily while I was doomed to paddle along with this enormous weight pulling down on my legs. The cramps in my legs and my abdomen were so bad that I woke up with a groan. It was not until after I had run to the bathroom for the necessary precautions against bloodstains on the sheets that I sat down to reflect on the contents of my nightmare.

My mother never had been in a swimming pool, never had learned how to swim, and never had been in the water with me. My mother lived 5,000 miles away and I had not seen her, nor talked to her, for several years. Yet, in some way it was true that my mother was a competent swimmer——in the waters of motherhood, that is. She had been incredibly healthy, and she had produced a child almost annually. Her motherhood was her career, and like any career which takes up all one's attention and energy, it was a successful career. Though gifted in many ways, she never questioned whether there were other things that a woman might want to do besides being a mother and wife.

However, the gentle way in which she embraced her motherly role did not deter her from instilling in my unformed conscience her open scorn and vehement condemnation of any female who did not fit unquestionably into the stereotypical motherly role. I remembered too well her vivid criticism of those women who held whatever measly jobs that were available at the time in economically-depressed Flanders. And because mother also talked about those who remained childless with such vehement derision, the hardened memory of it still haunted me in my dreams. Had she but known that her biting scorn for those who were childless would come to weigh down on me at a time when she would no longer be in a position to explain or lessen her contempt. Her beliefs and the way she communicated them to me tormented my dreams for the best part of my biologically productive years.

Added to the absence through distance that lay between us, an absence which in my pain I had translated as rejection, there now was the added condemnation of those who, like me, remained childless. Because I hurt miserably, I clung desperately to my distorted and childish vision of the mother I barely remembered as the perfect mother. It was not until I guiltily began to hate her, and every picture of her in my house, that I stopped believing that her rejection and contempt for me were justified. However, the trade-off was hardly worth it. Added to my feelings of abandonment and loneliness were now also those of guilt and self-reproach.

My mother would surprise me in the end. She would accept my children as her favorite grandchildren, once I could afford to go and visit. I could not help thinking how much self-torture could have been avoided if only we had not lived at such great distance from each other, and if only she had made an effort to stay in touch by letter or by phone. Just as the lack of communication between me and my in-laws had caused many a drawn-out misunderstanding, my distance from my parents also caused me much unnecessary grief.

The same kind of needless anguish was caused by my overprotective attitude to Daniel. I had simply and quietly taken the blame for not being able to conceive. If our childlessness was the result of Daniel's infertility, I did not want him to know. He would be devastated, I thought. I have often since cursed those taboos that make it a woman's job to protect her husband's ego. I was not supposed to fall apart because people were always trying to "fix" my childlessness, but I was to keep my husband from feeling less than a man. It was to be several years before we discovered that infertility ran in Daniel's family.

I also felt that my husband did not appreciate my need to choose, to decide freely in matters concerning fertility, so that for a long time I lived with the searing conflict between wanting to be my own person, and blaming myself for not being the fruitful vine of the patriarchs. I remember how I sometimes groaned inwardly when yet one more well-meaning person gave me the name of her doctor. I wanted to be accepted for the person that I was, and not treated as a problem which needed to be solved.

Daniel, too, surprised me, in the end. Quite content and proud now, with his little daughter and son, he no longer cared how these children had come into his life. All he knew was that he was a very happy father. His happiness allowed him to be a far better parent than my deflated self-esteem would permit me to be.

The children brought their own demands and their own joy. Because of all the emotional confusion in my life so far, however, I felt ill equipped for the emotional demands of motherhood. I had already become too confused by life, and too fearful of love and hurt. To love, to me, meant to be hurt. And I was not going to be hurt ever again. The children's and Daniel's happiness only served to highlight my own inner sadness and feelings of inadequacy. I could not share in their happy little world. I could only think of the time that these children, too, would leave me, or turn against me, or become estranged from me. My whole experience with human relationships had taught me that every time I had given my heart to someone, something had happened to bring the relationship to a disastrous end. To protect myself, I remained aloof from my children. To protect them against the pain of loss that had become staple to my own life, I concentrated on helping them grow into independence. I believed that if they were sure and independent they would not be hurt by the fickleness of human relationships.

One day in December, I was in the only place where I ever really felt at home, a plane halfway across the Atlantic. There I did not feel the tug and pull between the two countries that tore at my divided loyalties. It was now six years after I had left Belgium and I was taking the children to visit their grandma for the first time. Timmy had dozed off as soon as we had been airborne and after dinner Mary Elisabeth, too, curled up on the floor of the plane and fell asleep. My husband had reluctantly stayed behind to look after the cows. Fortified by Wardair's dusk-to-dawn bar, I exchanged cigarettes and confidences with the stranger in the seat next to me.

When Timmy woke up, he rubbed the sleep out of his eyes, and looked through the window and pointed down at the clouds below. "Mom, what's that white stuff?" he asked in a voice still full of sleep. "Those are the clouds, honey!" I said. "Down there!" he exclaimed. Clouds were supposed to be up in the sky above, not in the sky below.

While I kissed his sleepy face, I mused. The heavy clouds that had been blocking the sun from my vision would have to be transcended. Just as the airplane had been invented to cross the Atlantic, so I would have to devise ways and means to transcend the rules and taboos which kept me imprisoned. But just then, the night had been too lonely, and the road toward transcendence had been too long. The depression which had descended on me a few months earlier would persist intermittently for years to come. It did not reveal itself as the suppressed rage that it was, until after many more years of searching and studying.

I sensed so deeply the struggles behind me and the challenges ahead of me. I wanted to stop the world and get off, but for the next two weeks, I let the warmth and affection of my family flow over me like the warming rays of the sun, and its effect was therapeutic. And I thanked once again the amazing grace of the cosmos that always seemed to nourish me and keep me going onto that most difficult of all journeys, the journey into the self.

Chapter Five

Roses in the Desert

Where it began I can't begin to know it but then I know it is growing strong.[2]

Neil Diamond's voice, coarse and emotional, flowed from the little radio as I quickly and efficiently attached the milkers to the steady line-up of cows coming through the milking parlor.

It was in the spring, the spring became the summer, who would've believed you'd come along.

Neil Diamond espoused for me all the raw invincible emotion of the street kid, emotion which I had always been taught to suppress. Today, I was Sweet Carolyn, and sweet Carolyn was in love for the second time in her life.

I did not know just when and where it had begun.

That year in March, this country had really lived up to its reputation of being the land that God gave to Cain. Six long months of winter refused to give way to spring. Half of our calves refused to live. I tried throwing ice cold water over their head, I slapped them, held them upside down, tried to breathe air in their nostrils, but to no avail. John, one of our vets came out day or night, whenever we called. He administered vitamins, vaccine, bottled calcium, and overall tender, loving care for animals and farmers alike, but still the pet food truck had come in daily to claim a corpse.

I was tired of death. I was tired to death.

John came in for an evening call. "How are you," I tried to say, noting with surprise how involuntarily my voice was dropping to a whisper.

"I am fine," came the too-gentle reply, as John's voice, too, was taking on that distinctive tender quality that never failed to argue an instant closeness between us.

Suddenly, my heart was pounding so hard that it was impossible to act normal, to be the farmer's wife speaking politely to the veterinarian. I took deep, slow breaths in an attempt to regain some control over the rush of excitement that the mere sight of him had caused.

"Great day, isn't it," he ventured once more in a wooden effort to regain control.

"The best," I said, realizing instantly that my words had taken on a double meaning.

"I wanted to see that cow again that had milkfever yesterday"; he was managing now, but this time the tone of his voice was several pitches too high.

"She is still in the maternity pen," I said, feeling somewhat more confident, reassured now that his feelings for me were just as tumultuous as my feelings for him.

Stay with me for awhile, talk to me, hold me, make love to me.

I waited for John to come back. Ten minutes later, he came in to wash off his boots, but when I went to ask him about the patient I was annoyed that my voice once again sounded forced and mechanical. "How is she?" I said, meaning the cow.

"I might come back tomorrow to give her another bottle of calcium," he said. His manner had suddenly become too harsh and too abrupt.

"Hurray for normalcy and decency," I thought, cynically.

Here I am, the dutiful wife, and all I want is to get laid. And all he wants is to get laid.

And where in the hell can we go?

I did not know exactly when my desire to live, to love, and to be connected had erupted into an emotional volcano. It probably had been in that Spring, when the hard and long winter had finally given way at last to new life, new energy, and new hope.

But now I remember the night, and it don't seem so lonely we fill it up with only two. And when I hurt, hurting runs off my shoulders, how can I hurt when I am holding you.

Neil Diamond's song, and every other love song were suddenly filled with meaning again, changing the messages of death and despair into promises of love and joy. I was transported into an experience that I had not even learned to name. Spring and summer of that year I, too, felt that good times had never seemed so good. And I, too, had been inclined to believe they never would.

The flowers never bloomed so beautiful.
The grass never seemed so green.
The earth never felt so warm and soft.
The sunlight never so luminous.
Never again would I feel so beautiful,
never would love's nectar taste so sweet and so pure.

The universe had been created for a reason.
It spoke of John's glorious body,
his blue eyes, his loving face.
Enjoy it, you may never experience such
marvels again as long as you live!

The spring became the summer and there were to be many more times like these. I would watch John while he was expertly doing a Caesarian section on a cow at two o'clock in the morning, and afterward, in the unbroken silence of the early morning, we would stand exhausted, together with Daniel, drinking the Irish coffee I had made. That following winter, I watched him from across the fireplace, a bottle of Canadian Club between us while we waited for a sudden blizzard to subside so that he could drive back to the clinic.

We danced at socials and receptions, and we left Daniel in a blissful ignorance that no man would be interested in anything else but work. Daniel may not have had a lover, but he sure had found the love of his life and it wasn't me. It was the farm. How could I ever compete with a mistress such as that? My main purpose for my being in his life just then, it seemed to me, was to help him with the farm.

* * *

It was the first space that I created for myself.

Marriage has often been called "the one great American idolatry," fulfiller of all dreams, answer to every need, the happily ever after. When Cupid struck, it seemed to me to be appropriate punishment for such idolatry.

Given that one has the chance to fall in love only twice or thrice during the course of one's life, here I was given the second of my three chances.

I would not dare compare the different times that I fell in love, however, because each time I learned something from the previous experience. And, as with reading a book that one has read before, each time there were things that I wanted to explore more fully, while there were parts that I wanted to skip because I know them too well already.

Compared to my first instance of falling in love, this boundary crasher was a quantum leap. When I had fallen in love with Daniel at 16, it had been the most natural thing between me and the boy next door. I had been in love with life then, with the people in my life, so that it seemed no big deal to be falling in love with a young man seven years my senior. It was a natural progression on the road to maturity and everyone had been supportive of it. I had felt loved and secure then, and to meet someone with whom I wanted to share my life was only an extension of what went before.

This second time around, however, I neither had security nor support. My emotional life had become unraveled steadily over the past years, and the falling in love may well have been a creative attempt of my unconscious to gather up the pieces of my life and make some sense out of it.

On the one hand, I was afraid to become emotionally involved with anyone for fear that I would get hurt again, and I was eager to find excuses not to have to make friends; on the other hand, I became obsessed with the experience of "being in love." I needed very strong doses of caring and special attention to heal the ego pain with which I had been left, and I was looking for love and limerance to restore my self-esteem.[3] That the short-lived nature of these relationships with their imminent rejections and disappointments only served to lower my self-esteem further would become evident only much later.

But for now, I only knew that I had enough pain, and that I badly needed some joy. I had enough of the hardening fear and apathy in myself, now I wanted to feel loving again. And even if this experience was an emotional roller coaster of too few highs and way too many lows, it was occurrences such as these that kept my life from becoming a story of despair.

The only thing that I had been taught on falling in love was that falling in love is an invitation to love, but that it in no way constitutes real love. But then, I had been preparing for marriage, and not for falling in love with a friend, a colleague, a patient, or a boss. The psychotherapists, the priests, and the counsellors had not as yet written the chapter on the pains and joys, the dangers and benefits of falling in love, and if even they had, I had not read it. Nevertheless, I clung to the little wisdom that I had.

Those first years of my marriage, I, too, had still believed that marriage was to be the answer for everything, the happy-ever-after of the fairy tales. Therefore, I was laboring under several myths and misconceptions.[4] One of these myths, the myth of romantic love, implies that there is only one man meant for a woman and only one woman for a man and that this is predetermined in the stars. Once we find the right man or woman we will then be able to satisfy all each other's needs. In a perfect marriage, we believed, there would be no needs left unfulfilled, hence there would be no need for anyone else, and certainly there would be no need for another woman, or another man. I regarded marriage as the sacramentalized perpetuation of romantic love, and if one was attracted to, or fell in love with someone outside the marriage, one had to resist such "temptation." Or, one must look for the deficiencies in the marriage itself, since it was only in a failing marriage that one would have cause to look for fulfillment elsewhere.

Because of this myth of romantic love that taught me that I should find complete fulfilment in marriage, I was confused and scared. However, with Daniel work came first, and I was there to help him with the work. This, and his emotional involvement with one of his brothers who had moved next door to us by now, left me with a feeling of betrayal. My struggling identity eclipsed by theirs, I could not have work that was mine, no friends that were mine, no relatives that were mine. All I had that was mine was a huge inheritance of misunderstanding, confusion, pain and loss.

As is the case with many young couples, we believed that love meant that we had to think alike, feel alike, believe the same things, and be interested in the same things. I felt that I should love the things that Daniel loved, be interested in the things that Daniel did, and I felt badly when I didn't. Mostly, I felt bad about wanting to be a person in my own right. The result was that in spite of having two children, I was aware of such absurd emptiness inside me that I could almost hear its reverberating sound.

It was in an attempt to become a person in my own right that I clung to John. He did not judge me, try to change me, or try to box me in. In fact, the experience of being in love taught us how people are constantly judging each other, attempting to change each other, trying to box each other in. Falling in love, on the other hand, was an invitation to openness and unconditional acceptance. In short it was an invitation to love.

It was a lonely journey, however. In this culture, friendships between people of the opposite sex, platonic or otherwise, were still frowned upon. They could not even take on a formal structure such as a friendship between a professor and student, a therapist and a client, a brother and a sister, or a priest and a parishioner. Even in such formal relationships, pioneers were still trying to understand the connection between love and sex, the link between genuine loving and physical attraction. Experts all over were still struggling to define the rules of the game.

Meanwhile, while I was coping with these questions that experts feared to touch, farming was still largely a man's world, and I could not wait for the experts, I needed to live now. To most people, these questions did not matter. The man's world of the business of farming was well complemented with family and community events. Family and community ties gave ample room to most women to give meaning to their work and life. But I had no family, then, and was not as yet comfortable in nor accepted as a member of the community. Perhaps if I had a sister, a mother, a brother, or a friend to be loyal to me, to be concerned about me, to help me feel secure in my own identity, that would have been enough for me.

Yet, I wonder now, if I had had a variety of relationships in which I could have extended myself, would they have been enough for me? Once I had transcended one culture, it was impossible to become unquestioningly part of another. I would always be caught between my need to belong and my desire to examine, question, analyze, experiment, understand and transcend the makings of a culture. Once cultural taboos and rules are seen in their relativity, they can never again be accepted without question.

However, I did not really understand what was happening to me then. All I knew was that my world had fallen apart, and that I found most ordinary socializing unrewarding. I discovered in the secrecy of John's love a depth which enabled me to tolerate with greater ease the many social events which I found alienating and much too superficial.

My first reaction toward falling in love had been one of self-righteous superiority to my own feelings and to the man who was so very much taken with me.

> *Who the hell did I get that from? Who had told me that feelings should be classified as good or bad? Who said that being in love was good in certain circumstances and bad in others? Who said that sexual feelings only belonged in marriage?*

Raised as a good Catholic, I had always given over the interpretation of any part of my sexual conduct and feeling to the priest in private confession. As the French philosopher Michel Foucault so compelling argued, in the pre-Vatican II Church in which I grew up, sexuality was the medium for exercise of ecclesiastical power. The Church defined what was legitimate and established penalties for sexual conduct. The result was extreme self-consciousness about one's sexual conduct and estrangement from the most personal, intimate part of one's own life. Some love was sanctioned, and some was not. It was between fidelity to my own intimate feelings and experiences, and the sanctioning power of the church that my inner battles would be fought in the next few years.

I had just returned from a one-week retreat on renewal in my parish church, a project called Renewal 1967, and my heart, which had closed down in fear and hurt and bitterness toward all human beings because of my experiences with my family and in-laws, had become soft once again. The week of Renewal had strengthened in me confidence in myself and my own faith. More than ever I felt that my salvation rested, not in individual piety, but in relation to others, and I was willing to struggle with whatever lay before me. I was willing to learn to live by my own conscience, my own values, and not simply the hand-me-downs that my parents and my Church had given me.

Foolishly, considering what went before, I was again willing to take the leap in the cool, swirling waters of the unknowns of human relationships. In some ways, I was like a construction foreman who was to build a structure without a blueprint. Like all young entrepreneurs who walk where angels fear to tread, I, too, was determined to prove that I could deal with whatever problem that would come up, so, even though the experience of falling in love is something that fatefully happened to me, I made the deliberate decision to let it happen. I was willing to take the plunge into the unknown.

It is difficult to describe my own reasons for being in love with John, just as it would be difficult to describe his. There was of course the romantic element. Even without my hormone-enhanced vision, I could see that he was good-looking. He had a quality of at-oneness about him that people possess who have a no-nonsense relationship with nature. He also had that peculiar tenderness of those who work with animals. But it was his almost embarrassing honesty which made my artificially-bred sham philosophy be exposed for what it was, a legacy of my upbringing which only served the purpose of escaping life. Best of all, John took me seriously, and it was in the middle of a rather heated argument that suddenly I realized that he was more important to me than the issue that we were so dead set on arguing about.

In the months that followed, the glory and the mud, the light and the shadows of the relationship were so intertwined that it took constant analysis on my part to understand what was happening. During that first year, my initial caution grew into a desire and longing so real that it became a constant physical ache. If my first love had been made in heaven, than certainly this one was more like pure hell.

By Christmas of that year, the new birth already began to show itself as a death. Hearing the sound of church bells chiming had once again made me aware of how badly I missed the sounds of Europe. Seeing families flock into church for Midnight Mass only served to remind me of the family that I had lost. I had listened to the ancient ritual and I was once again reminded that my Church could give me comfort no longer. I had gone to bed, and listening to the sound of the voices of the people in the living room noisily celebrating Christmas Eve, I felt disconnected and alone. My pain would have been intolerable if I had not had a fantasy of John making love to me in a moment of passion and fusion. If Daniel had succeeded in taking me away from my loved ones, my love for John made me feel that in the whole world, I had at least one friend who found me special and worthwhile.

Even though the relationship was to remain unresolved for years, the intense struggle of conscience only lasted a few months. That winter, I was reading Georges Vanier's little volume, *In weakness strength*. It read, and I knew the passage by heart from one of the letters of St. Paul:

> *My Son, when the Lord corrects you, do not treat it lightly, but do not get discouraged when he reprimands you. Suffering is part of your training. God is treating you as his sons. . .Of course punishment is most painful at the time and far from pleasant, but later in those in whom it has been used it bears fruit in peace and greatness. . .so hold up your limp arms and steady your trembling knees and smooth out the path you tread; that injured limb will not be wrenched, it will grow strong again.*[5]

> *The message was for God's sons only. In those days, She didn't have any daughters yet.*

I took it to be good advice for God's daughters, too. I believed it with all my heart, but the unceasing agony of it all only drove me more desperately to want to be in John's arms, wanting to be safe, to be secure, to be comforted, to be loved. After this, no friendship with any man would ever have the same intolerable physical intensity. It was an intensity of such amplitude that it frightened me and forced me to try to understand the mystery of my own self.

> *I will never suffer this way again! If only because no one ever suffers and agonizes with the same intensity and in quite the same way twice.*

> *Or maybe because, having caught this vicious virus*
> *once, I would be inoculated against the severity of its*
> *impact for ever after.*

There were a host of ways in which I tried to rationalize why my relationship with John could never become an affair, but to this day the colossal struggle that was involved in staying out of bed still does not seem worth it. I can sympathize now with the therapist or psychologist who has the enormous discipline and insight not to get sexually involved with a patient, but when the same challenge was put to me, I lacked support, insight, and education. I was left to deal with such a situation alone. The long-term frustration, and what amounted to daily psychological torture, could not help taking its toll.

If I had to make a virtue out of necessity, I never really felt virtuous about it all. John and I simply did not live in the kind of environment where having an affair would go unnoticed. I knew that it would just as surely have been condemned by all, so we did not actively seek out occasions where we could be alone. If God wanted me to suffer through this experience to arrive at some new insight, so be it.

I often questioned, however, what kind of God would stand by and let human beings expire in their own pain. It was no accident then that in the still distant future I was .to write my Master's thesis on the question of suffering.

Therefore, I stuck by my own philosophy, that if I did not know the answers to the questions of life, there was nothing to stop me from loving the questions. If infidelity was harmful to a marriage, I had to know why. I could not simply take someone else's word for it that it was. I wanted to decide what was right for me in my situation, pulling together the strands of commitments and responsibilities of my own life. Finally, some of the answers at least started to come.

I knew that love I must, that I could not confine my love to one person, and make that person my whole life, but I also realized that I was spreading myself too thin. I learned that someone would eventually get hurt if I tried to love more than one man at the same time. I also learned that I was not willing to destroy anyone else's life in the pursuit of my own happiness and fulfillment. I had to travel to the brink of agony before I could say, "I do not want to sleep with you, not because I love you too little, but because I love you too much, not because I am afraid of what people would say, not because I am afraid of what would happen, but because I know that what would happen is that I could do you no justice. I would always be torn between you and my husband, and I do not want to love one and vilify the other."

So it happened, that amidst the hundred and one good reasons to have an affair, and an equal number of good reasons not to, I agonized endlessly over the rightness of love and the wrongness of unfaithfulness. In the end, it was the rightness of love that kept me going. My world opened up in a way that is difficult to describe. I was able to welcome to my world someone who was old enough to be my father. I learned to think of someone who was a parent as a person in his own right. Until then I had thought of parents as people who exist solely for the comfort of their children. I learned to see life through the eyes of someone who was experiencing the crises of the middle years. Tired of the incessant demands of adult children, John was searching for the meaning and purpose of his life. In that sense, we were closer in age than we thought. Had I not had too many demands placed on me by my "teenage" brothers-in-law? Had I not done my duty, what was expected of me, while no one had asked about "me"? Yet, many of his reasons for being in love were to remain obscure to me. Being in love was simple fact and it needed no reasons to justify it.

It was easier for me to analyze what my reasons were for loving him. He was someone who had been born in Canada, and who was as intimately tied to this country as I had been to mine. It was his rootedness in this country that I wanted for myself. I had never had the same feeling of at-oneness with Canada as I had with Belgium. If any words could describe those first years in Canada, it would be the words "disconnected," "displaced," and "uprooted." My relationship with John gave me back that feeling of being connected, rooted and in the right place. His tenderness and caring replaced the tenderness and caring of my parents that I missed so badly. I loved him in the same way that I would have loved my parents, only my love grew immeasurably more mature. Because of my love for John, I learned to love Canada as my own country, and Canadian people as my own. In short, because of my love for John, I became rooted in Canada.

As an additional bonus, John's language, which was English, and thus had been a foreign language to me, now became the language of an intimate. Before, the only tongue in which I spoke to an intimate was Flemish. English was the language that I reserved for formal and business conversations. My culture, which had been my handicap, expanded to welcome the culture that I had embraced by immigration. Partly because I was confused at the intensity of my need for him, and partly because his otherness pointed at a larger world which I had as yet to explore, I began to read many publications which opened up to me a world outside my Catholic culture. I also sought to broaden the horizons of my own Catholic culture.

Of course, I also matured sexually. Even though I was not able to sleep with John, there was nothing to prevent me from fantasizing about the delights of sexual love. Fantasy is one of the best aphrodisiacs to be found. My marital sex life became more exciting as a result. Just as the Church sanctioned sex in marriage and through this sanctioning set boundaries to what was sanctioned, so unsanctioned sex had the power to liberate marital sex from any artificially-set parameters. However, my sexual freedom was to be painstakingly gained. It would take no less than a twenty-year journey before I would actually be free from guilt, from misgivings, and from anxieties regarding my own sexuality. Many years later, when my own daughter had her first love affair, and my husband was most critical of her, I struck him in anger. "Don't you dare hang the same self-condemning sexual baggage around her neck as we had hung around our necks when we grew up." Never again did Daniel dare criticize her after that.

Moreover, in claiming my deepest emotions once again, I became a better mother. Once I had to kill off my emotions toward my family because the feelings of abandonment had gotten to be much too painful to bear. Yet if I was to raise children, I needed these feelings. My relationship with John helped me in some odd way to regain my loving feelings.

I also learned to live with a world of doubt, of not knowing what the purpose or the outcome of this relationship would be. I learned what it meant to tolerate the darkness of not knowing.

> *I said to my soul, be still, and let the dark come upon you, which shall be the darkness of God.*[6]

Most important, though, in John's unwavering loyalty amidst the confusion of the impossibility of our relationship, my faith in humanity was renewed. For the time that it lasted, at least, I was to find in the loyalty of that secret love the feeling of continuity that I had lost some years earlier. I will always remember with gratitude this relationship which brought me closer to my self and my everyday life, and which powerfully propelled me far beyond it. My friendship with him moved me toward a greater freedom. With the floodgates of love wide open, I once again felt that I moved in a world of cosmic dimensions.

Today, my heart still swells at the memory of the agony and sweetness of that passion-filled interlude. Whenever I hear the words of that all-too-familiar song, "Help me make it through the night," I stop for a moment, and I am 24 again, dependent on the grace-filled cosmos to help me make it through the night. Years later, when the relationship finally and mercifully petered out, and all the urgency and the electricity, the magic and romance had gone out of it, this temporary collapse of my ego boundaries had resulted in a permanent growth of self so that I would now be able to include in my world with greater comfort and ease those who were to become my friends and my teachers in my new country.

It was shortly after I had taken the children to visit my parents for the first time that I let go of my intense emotional attachment to John. I had regained some sense of being connected to my family of origin during this two-week stay, at which the children had also been welcomed by my parents with open arms, but I had also become acutely aware of the limitations of their love. Till then, I had retained a fantasy that a parental figure could give security, understanding and support.

But now I realized that, much as I had enjoyed the temporary affection my relatives bestowed on me, I had nevertheless outgrown them. They could no longer provide me with that security, comfort, and understanding that I so craved. The best they could do was remind me of that part of my identity that was tied up with them. Being keenly aware of the many challenges and decisions of my own life, I realized that there were too many things that I would have to face alone. It was a profoundly humbling experience to realize that I could not take on the responsibility of other people's lives, that I had enough with myself to care for.

The reunion and togetherness in Belgium that I had so longed for resulted once more in a profound awareness of my aloneness and separateness upon my return to Canada. I was different from either one of the cultures that I knew so well, Canadian or Belgian. I felt then that we must live alone and die alone; that in all the important moments of life, we are alone. I knew the richness and terror of the place where one experiences the burden of one's uniqueness, and where one humbly accepts one's limitations, along with the limitations of others.

> *The courage to be alone? It comes from being pushed to that place—at first most unwillingly, in suffering and terror, then after many times, with understanding, then in peace many times, and finally in joy, then forgetting, and beginning again in suffering and terror. . .*[7]

I could now see my friendship with John in a different light, and I was able to become less emotionally entrapped. For a time, at least, we had been able to enrich each other with our love, but now I knew the limits of what we could be to each other. The initial sensation of freedom that followed my disentanglement from him, however, was soon followed by intense grief at the loss of a lover. I was not prepared for the long process of grieving that was awaiting me. My husband could no longer ignore this monumental grief, and this, along with my seemingly cold attitude toward his friend John, mystified and annoyed him. Just as John and I had once marvelled at our closeness, we were now biting each other's head off as if to try to regain some distance between us. Surprisingly, it was the violence with which we snapped at each other that finally tipped off Daniel and John's wife to the nature of our relationship. They had not known the intensity of our enmeshment until they watched it break into splinters. It was in an attempt to deal with my grief and the baffling break in John's friendship that Daniel learned about the extent of our emotional involvement.

Chapter Six

In Search of Understanding

I listened intently to the handsome young man with dark hair and intense, brown eyes swimming with emotion. He spoke of love, of life, of the Holy Spirit. It was Pentecost at St. Michael's Church. The priest, Father Rob, had just been appointed to this parish and his homily was filled with enthusiasm and promise. His words were like balm on my weary spirit, and a flicker of new hope began once again to burn inside me.

It was during the emotional high of my love for John that I had switched parish churches. I had gone there on my way home from the hospital emergency room, after taking one of the children in for treatment of a minor burn. The singing had been beautiful, the preaching fired my imagination, and the whole atmosphere had been peaceful and reviving.

It was only a year after a program of renewal at my local parish church, a time during which I had been filled with a new hope, with faith, with love, and with common sense, but afterwards this parish seemed to have returned to its previous pattern of dead formalism, so that I could not find anything there that would speak to my imagination or help me make sense out of my life.

After those first inspired reverberations of Vatican II which had so hopefully begun with the new culture of theologians, bishops and priests, many Catholics drifted back into the old familiar ways, not ready to assume responsibility for the direction of their church. The result was that this parish church remained a strange mixture of the power of institutionalized death and institutionalized life.

For most people in this farm community, going to church on Sunday remained an integral part of the farm life. After Mass, renewed by prayer and the celebration of the Eucharist, the farm people stood around and shared news, gossip, and common concerns. I had always felt a need for more than I could find there, but every attempt to address this need had left me cold and shivering with disappointment, the smell of death lingering in my nostrils. I also managed to feel acutely guilty because I did not seem to belong. After all, hadn't my whole upbringing been geared toward this sense of belonging which comes from thinking alike, feeling alike, agreeing on the same things, sharing the same traditions and the same rituals?

So on this day I found myself sitting in this smooth, shiny wooden pew, hoping that somehow a different parish church would have more to offer.

My instincts proved to be right.

The two priests that had just come to St. Michael's were both excellent preachers who were eager to express through the liturgy the many humanizing qualities of Vatican II. Father Roy was a theologian and eloquent lecturer, and young Father Rob, fresh out of seminary, was equally dedicated to his work.

For the next two years I was to find great comfort in attending this church, especially during the Canadian winters, which still seemed unduly harsh and long to my Flemish sensibilities. Here I could find an escape from the interminable mess of snow and mud and manure which cluttered my surroundings in the barn and what was then still our old house. With the constant demands of husband and children and farm, I also benefited from the time of peace and quiet that I could find before or after Mass, away from the noise and the depressing disarray at home.

There I also found a kind of community to assuage my loneliness. This, along with the togetherness that we experienced at our monthly dances at the Belgian-Dutch-Canadian Club, and the happiness of our Sunday excursions to the lake with the children, I was able to forget, temporarily at least, my problem-ridden existence. I learned how to cope, even if I had not learned how to resolve.

It was not that I did not continue trying, but I knew that even if I found temporary relief from my own inner pain in the structured atmosphere of my religion, there was that part of me that knew that I could never go back to a life of conformity and non-freedom. However, at this point I had no way of moving ahead either. I could not seek and find answers that fit the size of my questions. I could not find enough pieces to begin to be able to fit them together somehow to make sense of my experience. Yet, somehow I perceived that here I could find some glimpses, and for now I had to be content with that.

Nevertheless, it often appeared to me that other people had a handle on their lives that I did not have. Other people, who did all the same things that I did, were happy and fulfilled. As a result I was beginning to see my restless search and the chaos in my life as a consequence of my own failures.

Religion was supposed to give me insight and peace, not turmoil and chaos.

Yet, all my experiences had resulted in more questions than answers, more sadness than joy, more turmoil than peace. Certainly, I thought, I must be a very bad Christian to be carrying so much guilt and ambivalence. Most of all, I could not reconcile my persisting sadness with faith and hope.

> *When the night has been too lonely,*
> *and the road has been too long;*
> *some may think that love is only*
> *for the lucky and the strong.*[8]

In retrospect, I can see that many of my guilt feelings were caused by traditional Western stereotyping which said that females should be compliant but discerning, inconsistent and irrational, illogical but intuitive, content to live through others and, therefore, happy with the goal of becoming a loving mother. Hindsight also tells me that my feelings of anger and guilt were at the same time the result of not being able to share so much of myself with anyone. I could not bear so much secrecy, so much hiddenness from others. I needed to be able to clarify my own values and decide what was important to me. I had to express myself in my being different from others. I had to be assertive so as to take charge of my life. I needed to understand intellectually as well as emotionally. I needed to sort out and organize the jumble of my existence in a logical way. I would have welcomed a competent therapist who could help me to illuminate both the best and worst in me.

As it was, I had been taught that the only place that deep dark secrets belong are in the confessional, so when I got depressed I went to confession, and when I fell in love I went to confession. Then I got more depressed. What I needed was an open and honest relationship. The kind of thing people talked about but few people, as yet, seemed to know how to carry out successfully. I was convinced, then, that it was this kind of relationship that I would need to regain my zest for living and my confidence in the future.

For as long as any attempt at communication seemed to be doomed to failure, I had no choice but to close down. I lived those parts of myself that others could identify with, but without any prospects of happiness or fulfillment.

Because whole parts of myself remained unclaimed and my feelings of guilt, conscious or unconscious, continued to increase, I could find little satisfaction in my role as wife and mother. Not that my role of wife and mother or farm woman did not have any potential for self-fulfillment, it did, but the rejected part of myself would not allow me to find fulfillment in the role of wife and mother, either.

* * *

Because I had felt increasingly as if I would soon explode with the heaviness of my many secret conflicts, needs, and emotions, and also because I felt I needed to share with someone the immense struggle that lay behind me now, I had told my husband about my relationship with John. After his initial kindness and empathy, he had understandably become upset. The distress between us spiralled until I was unable to function any longer.

I felt more than ever that moralizing and rationalizing one's way through life was useless, and that everything was a matter of personal responsibility and decision-making, but those who were willing to struggle with difficult situations and decisions are a rare breed, and those who are capable of providing guidance and insight seemed impossible to find. Certainly, the moralists and philosophers and those who deal only with abstractions could not be of any help to me.

Confession had proved to be a band-aid treatment for an ailment that required skillful and long-term therapy. It merely confronted me with my own understanding of the complexities of the human psyche which no amount of institutionalized legalism or penal system could cover. Good counselling was hard to come by, and I felt as if I was up against a wall of ignorance, some of it awkward and some of it arrogant.

In an act of desperation, after having come to an emotional deadlock with Daniel, I had gone to see Father Rob.

Take one Catholic priest who has made a commitment to teach Catholic moral values only. Add one Catholic woman whose subconscious referee goads her to live up to the Catholic Ideal. Add a marriage counsellor who cannot hide his disdain for religious values from his client. Top it off with a husband who both envies and fears his wife's freedom, and who sees this freedom as a cause of her guilt. The result is four negatives and no positives, a recipe for disaster.

I had dressed carefully in the new canary yellow slacks and tunic that I had made for myself, noticing that it showed off my tan beautifully. Even though it was only the middle of June I looked as healthy and beautiful as any young woman who lived outdoors most of the time. In spite of the way I looked, I felt I was riding an emotional roller coaster and I would somehow crash any time.

Once in his office, Father Rob had pointed toward a chair, but I chose to stand. For the longest time, I stood there motionless and concentrating, as an athlete might stand while contemplating a decisive move.

Then came my first mistake. I tried to sound rational, avoiding all emotion. It was my intellectual self, telling the story of my intimate self. No confused welter of emotions showing here.

"It is kind of a long story," I ventured. "It will be difficult to make it short."

He turned his open honest gaze fully attentive towards me. "That's okay, take your time," he said.

My voice was clear and articulate, but somehow dissociated. It was someone else talking.

"Do you still want to love John?" Father Rob asked after I had finished speaking.

No, I don't want to love John, goddamnit. I want to make sense out of what has been happening to me. I want someone to say, "You did a hell of a good job on this one."

But then, what did I expect. He was at the beginning, I was in the middle of the course. And I wasn't there to teach him.

He was the one who was supposed to counsel me.

There was a long and awkward pause.

"Perhaps, you should see a marriage counsellor," he said finally.

"That's right," I thought desperately. "There must be something wrong with my marriage, otherwise I would not be in this predicament."

I tried one more time. Mistake number two.

"I pray about this every day, I read the Bible," I volunteered.

I felt even more vulnerable now that I had let this one out.

I sounded like a precursor of Tammy Baker.

I had been trying to fit together a life of prayer and the unrepressed emotions of being in love. I should have known then that Catholic men do not enter into seminaries to celebrate the mysteries of love between male and female. If they were trying so hard to separate prayer and love, who was I to try and put them together?

The long and sympathetic silences which enabled me to at least finish my story, and the sincere desire to help on the part of the priest, had left me somewhat comforted. Nevertheless, when I left his office, I felt as if I just had a tooth extracted without the benefit of novocaine.

In spite of that, I went to see him two more times. Once, Daniel even went with me.

And I did what I had always done best.

I idealized him. I was loyal, I was sympathetic, I was understanding, I was forgiving.

I lived vicariously through him. I mentally edited his sermons. I prayed with him and for him. That too was something that I did best. Did I not live for my husband and my children? One more did not make a difference. And it was the only way I knew how to stay attached and connected.

Then, Father Rob was moved to another parish.

Afterwards I even tried to contact him, but he did not answer my letters. He did not want to talk to me.

Much later, when I entered the seminary, I knew why.

I was a Negro trying to hang out with the Ku Klux Klan. If I had been middle-aged, fat and ugly, I may have had a chance. But I was too young, too beautiful, and if I wasn't the Virgin Mary, I had to be Eve. It was one or the other.

After the humanizing influences of Vatican II, the priest had to play old games by new rules, but he knew nothing of the new rules. They had changed the format of confessions to make counseling easier, but the only people who had unlimited access to a Ph.D. in human relations were the people who were married and had children, and the priest had neither.

It had been my love and admiration for this young priest that had given me the courage to confide in him. I had no blueprint by which to analyze either the priest's counseling competence nor my own emotional entrapment. I felt desperate, humiliated, a failure, and the very thought that this person, too, would not be able to be of any help to me had been unthinkable. I was too vulnerable and devastated to look for someone else.

Thus, I did what I always did best. I remained loyal, sympathetic, and forgiving. It was the only way that I knew how to stay attached and connected.

I also wrote a letter to Jean Vanier. I told him how much I enjoyed his books. Aboard a plane between Paris and London, he had time to answer my letter.

Someone did care!

And then there was John Powell. He too was out there writing books in the hope that others might be helped. He too answered my letter.

The Catholic culture was working. It was a two-edged sword.

Today, I am still angry when I think back now at my choice of counsellor, or perhaps it was lack of choice. Few priests were as yet trained to deal with marital and family problems, and even those who pioneered creatively in this area because of their desire to help were often caught between moral and philosophical abstractions, and their lack of familiarity with the struggles, choices and decision making of those who, like me, had to shape the destiny of their lives in the gaps that had been left by those very abstractions.

Meanwhile, my husband Daniel, who had come to resent my visits to Father Rob, was all too happy when the priest was moved to another parish. On the one hand, he feared that "Father's" attention to my person might give me some undeserved status in "the Church." In the parish, men were allowed to get some status and attention, but women were supposed to be in the kitchen making the coffee. Here, too, the Catholic culture was working. Here, too, it was a two-edged sword.

On the other hand, I was a possible source of embarrassment. In retrospect I can see, now, that Daniel was refereed by the same concepts of right and wrong that subconsciously bound me. As a result, he, too, saw my confusion as the result of too much freedom, too much guilty secrecy.

How was he to know that my anxiety was caused by too little self-revelation, too little feedback? Human relations were for educated people with nothing better to do. He was a farmer with more pressing things on his mind.

But farmer or priest, it was their love and caring that would have to justify them, and Daniel at least had no delusions about his ignorance. If he didn't understand, that was that. He loved me all the more in the ways that he knew how.

From professionals, however, I expected competence. Forever afterwards, whenever I was to hear a young and dedicated priest make the statement that "he wanted to help people," I would pray silently, "And may God help those that you will help." I had suffered too much pain in the discovery that this willingness to help was an eagerness matched only by incompetence.

What made many a seminarian ill-equipped to deal with those who, like me, wanted to live their lives in freedom and decisive choice was the same lack of freedom that kept Catholics from making their own choices and from tapping into their own competence or the expertise of professionals around them.

I had been set free into chaos, and in the chaos of my own freedom I was now looking for direction. I had had friends who assisted me in my personal growth, such as it was, before I came to Canada. European and North American societies were making progress toward greater freedom, emancipation, democratization, and humanization, and as a child of the 60s I had absorbed these influences. Yet, in my aloneness I was ill-equipped to create order of this exciting chaos that I had landed myself in. I knew little about the makings of Canadian society, or about channels that were open to me, and even those that I knew now filled me with fear and apprehension.

At the same time, I was also determined to be my own director. I was resolute to live the mystery of good and evil in my life. I may have been programmed to think that perfection meant the avoidance of sin, yet now I knew too well how intertwined good and evil were. If I was to be a doer, and not merely a talker, I would have to take the chance of plunging into life, with its ambiguity of good and evil, hoping that somehow I would gain a much deeper understanding and a much fuller life. Most of all I sensed that, as so many psychotherapists have pointed out all along, in order to be whole, to be complete, the darkness in me had to be functioning in harmony with every other part of me, and that it must not be rejected or split off.[9]

However, if during the 60s the Church was ill-equipped to deal with issues of human sexuality and human relationships, so was the modern world.

This too, I was soon to discover.

Shortly after my harrowing experience with Father Rob, I managed to make an appointment for both Daniel and myself with a marriage counsellor. Where the priest had retreated in sympathetic silence, the marriage counsellor clearly possessed the gift of gab. Each session with this man turned out to be an avalanche of words cascading down, beleaguering my already overworked mind. In three sessions he managed to communicate to me what seemed to be the contents of his master's degree in social work; his knowledge of Freud, his scepticism of religion, his views on incest and on oral sex. All these and more were presented to me simultaneously.

> *Shit! I must have looked intelligent—to invite such lengthy lectures! Or perhaps I just seemed free. There is nothing that seems to release a greater flow of creativity in a man than a free woman.*

Again, I felt that I was alone to wonder what all this had to do with me, or with my emotional crisis.

When Daniel came with me, the counsellor quickly analyzed my already-deflated husband as totally inadequate, since in his view, if I had a perfectly fulfilling marriage, there would be no need for me to fall in love with someone other than my husband. As he put it, "If you can find everything at K-Mart, why would you have to go shopping anywhere else?"

Neither did the marriage counsellor try to hide his disdain for Father Rob. He resented my loyalty to him. The doctor's hate of the shaman.

There proved to be something catharctic about this welter of ideas spilling over me, however. Maybe it reassured me that my brain at least was still in good working order. Still, it wasn't until, with a firm if imaginary kick, I booted the marriage counsellor out of my life and joined Daniel in the work on the field that my confidence in myself began to return.

The work on the farm never waited for troubled human relationships to straighten themselves out. This too proved to be therapeutic. Rather than being stuck in the dysfunction of my emotional life, I invested all my energy into the farm. In addition, the sessions had made Daniel more aware of his vulnerability, and for the time being I felt loving and needed, with the result that our relationship was strengthened. In relationship to the farm and the farmer, at least, I felt strong. But to my already full menu of distrusts and dislikes, I had now added my doubts and misgivings toward counsellors, educators, and social workers. The unfortunate spinoff was that my relationship with Daniel regressed to what it had been before, a fused relationship between two immigrants afraid of the larger world.

Meanwhile, I kept on going to the same church where the new pastor now preached his beautiful sermons, while I continued to sit in the pew, feeling increasingly like Mary Magdalen, my only possible status in the Church being that of a sinner, and not even a very good one at that.

I had enough of frustration, of disappointment, and of hopelessness. I was ready to conform to whatever it took to regain my peace. If I could find no way to put together the magnificent puzzle of life, at least I could retreat into conformity and compliance.

My religious beliefs had always given me a sense of identity that went back to my parents and family of origin. But that identity was only a tiny part of myself. I had no way to validate the larger experiences of falling in love, of deep and life-giving friendship, of seeking to know and understand, of the pain of separation, of emotional upheaval, in short of being acutely involved with life. There were whole parts of me that I could not claim and I felt alone in my loneliness.

> *When you love someone and you are separated from*
>   *them,*
> *nothing can fill the emptiness of absence.*
> *Do not even try to fill it,*
> *but simply accept and persevere.*
> *This seems hard, but it is a consolation,*
> *because as long as the emptiness remains,*
> *you remain connected with each other.*
> *Do not say that God fills the emptiness,*
> *because God does not. On the contrary,*
> *God keeps the emptiness open to help us preserve*
> *our earlier connectedness with each other.*
> *Be it a connectness in pain.*[10]

Often I woke up during the night and I could feel the loneliness well up inside me like a salt spring. I think that I would have welcomed the devil himself if he had offered me friendship and understanding. Fortunately for me, the mystic in me did not quit. My religious faith had proved to be a two-edged sword. Having no script to deal with the many upheavals in my life, I found the larger blueprint of my faith. Just as it is easier to see a distant light in the darkness of the night, so I could see clearly the all-embracing love of my Creator and my Redeemer. I am sure that it was during this time that Mary Magdalen's song in "I know that my Redeemer lives" became the motivational stance of my life.

It was words of hymns like these during Mass that communicated to me the faith of those men and women who had gone before me. Men and women who, no doubt, were involved in their own struggle toward health and wholeness. The symbolic words and symbolic acts of the Mass pointed to that Reality without which, at this moment at least, there was no longer any other reality for me.

My increased awareness of the mystery of good and evil in all of life allowed me to see preachers, theologians, counsellors and therapists alike as human beings who were only toying, often rather arrogantly, with bits and pieces of a larger truth, so much of which was beyond them. I could see how too many of them were satisfied to absolutize their little corner of truth. It was this need to absolutize parts of the truth which closed their minds to the power of love itself.

The more I became baffled by life, the more I sensed the greatness of the mystery of all human life. The more I felt that I did not belong to any culture, the more I felt myself to be a member of the whole of the human community. Most of all, the more I felt that I had lost everything that was ever important to me, the more I felt I had gained wisdom and insight in what theologians describe as "wholly other," the life of God, Herself.

Early that same summer, I stumbled on some tulip bulbs that had lain forgotten in the dark basement, because no one had remembered to plant them. Spindly yellow-green leaves had begun to climb alongside the wall toward the cellar window. In the heat of the sunlight outside, everything else was already in glorious bloom. But these forgotten bulbs had reached despairingly toward whatever little light seeped into the dank cellar. They had grown to a ridiculous length, determined to find the light. How symbolic those pathetic spindly leaves were of my own determined search for light, and growth and love. I stood there for a long time, reflecting on a plant's will to live. I knew then that a human being, too, can suffer in anxiety, fear, loneliness, guilt, rejection, deprivation and hopelessness, but that life is stronger than death, and that the human spirit is indomitable.

Chapter Seven
The Gift of the Land

I dropped the chains in my left pocket and their handles in my right and with hands trembling with nervous excitement I pulled on a pair of surgical gloves from the bottom shelf in the cupboard. I noiselessly climbed the steps to the maternity pen in the corner of the barn, and speaking gently to the animal hunched down against the side of the pen, I came as near to her as I dared, so as not to scare her away. The handsome head turned momentarily as the eyes took me in, and then, deciding that I was a familiar part of her world, the mother-to-be did not move.

"Good girl," I thought, "stay where you are."

Firmly, I took her tail in my left hand while sliding my right alongside the two legs of the calf, which were already protruding quite a ways with the tiny nose tucked neatly on top on them. I checked the size of the head which was stuck, tightly squeezed, still in the birth canal. Satisfied that the cow and I would manage together without any outside help, I slid one end of the chain over the one immaculate little hoof and the other end over the other. I could feel the huge body heave as the next contraction swept through the animal and I could see the calf's eyelids begin to flutter as it was reaching toward life outside the womb.

"What you need to assist a cow with calving is a nice big cigar," the old veterinarian had told me over the phone half an hour earlier. Sensing my anxiety, he had tried to put me at ease. The cigar was to help the farmer wait patiently while timing the animal's contractions. Unfortunately, neither cigars nor large animal veterinary work were as yet assigned to women then, so I had to do without the cigar and without precedents.

Yet I knew how to be patient. I knew how to go with the flow of contractions and short intervals of rest to let both the animal and myself regain enough strength so that she could push while I pulled hard on the chains. Momentarily, the head was painfully inching its way out, and I drew with all my strength, watching closely as the first half of the calf's body followed easily. After a small pause at the hips, the newborn slid onto the floor in front of me, sucking in a great breath of air and wiggling its wet little ears, and I, too, gave out a sigh of relief.

The farm had proven to be a lifesaver for me, even if I had not been born on a farm and had to learn everything from scratch. At first, the fields had seemed enormous, the machinery scary, and the responsibilities surrounding the care of animals overwhelming. Today, I had run back and forth to the kitchen window at least a dozen times, a nervous wreck looking for the veterinarian to drive up the lane. Having been tied up with other calls, he had only arrived after I had managed the job by myself. As usual, Daniel had been busy at the back end of the farm, finishing up a field, secure in his knowledge that I was here; that I would be here always.

The farm had become my life. It was a place where I felt competent. I got up with and went to bed with it. I carried it around like a snail her house. Sometimes I lost track of time, and began talking about time not in months and days, but I would speak of it as "seeding time," "haying time," "harvest time," "second cut" time, "silo filling time"; all these times separated only by little pit stops to gear up for the next "time." I too had grown annoyed at those people who remained uninitiated in this calendar year that farmers carry around in their psyche. Perhaps more than the new English language that I spoke, my parents were to hate my new "farmer's language" and my "farmer's psyche." I seemed to have joined another culture in more ways than one.

I also reluctantly began to relate to the farm as to a big business as I watched those initial small bank loans grow in size and in number. There were mortgages, quota loans, barn loans, silo and equipment loans. There were cash flows, budgets, business analyses and income projections. There were depreciation schedules, amortizations, long and short-term interest rates, wages, taxes and tax deductibles. This, too, was a language with which I had to become familiar. There were custom workers with expensive machinery doing the field work; there were a number of veterinarians doing monthly herd healths and emergency calls; and there were construction crews who were trying to squeeze another addition to a building here and there almost every summer.

Always there were lunches on the go: lunches in the kitchen, lunches in the office, lunches on the tractor, lunches in the yard, lunches on the tailgate of the truck, and lunches in the fields.

In the winter, there were the snowstorms, the frozen waterpipes, frozen silo unloaders, frozen feed, barn doors that had to be chipped loose every day. There was liquid manure that did not want to flow and solid manure which grew into too big a pile because the fields were covered with snow and there was no place to take it.

In the spring there were the desolate cold fields and the chilly winds. There was the tired bleak exhaustion after the illnesses of both the animals and their caretakers. However, there was also that first little bit of new hope without which we would not be able to begin to cultivate the soil and plant the seed, and then there was always and unfailingly the sudden burst of energy when nature exploded into a magnificent chorus of new life, renewing us all with her outpouring of new life. We could see our efforts rewarded when every seed planted began to sprout at once or in succession, and we knew that we had once again been allowed to do this demanding task as stewards of the land.

The summer quite often was the time when the farm was running us, and not the other way around. It was then that nature truly had us in her enchanted spell. The sun scorched us, the rain drowned us. If on certain days we could witness what we thankfully referred to as "a million dollar growth," we knew that these days would most certainly be followed by days when we would see the same growth devastated by a flood, a storm or a drought. Nature owed us and she owned us. She owned our worried hearts, our painful muscles, our tired bones, our aching souls. She had the power to make us or to break us. She was our wealth, our poverty, our joy, our despair. She was our greatest ally, but also our fiercest adversary. I learned to take her terrible power seriously, so that years later, when I began to attend seminars at the university concerning the ecology and the environment I could only despair at the naiveté of those who had never met that power face-to-face. As a farmer I would always be annoyed at the naive noncomprehension by the majority of people of those whom they sentimentally refer to as "the people of the land."

I had once been one of those proud and simple small farmers, and I remembered too well the long hours of hard soul-destroying labor which left no time for thought or reflection. When, after a long day in the field, a day of bravely suffering the bitter cold or the scorching sun, I came home to more work, to more hours of shovelling manure and feed for our "small" herd of less than 20 animals. When Daniel and I finally dropped down in bed exhausted, we knew only too well that tomorrow we would have to start over, if we could, that is. If I had any sentimental bones in my body before I became a farmer, I surely had none left now. It is not surprising that today, along with hundreds of my fellow farmers, I thank God every day for modern technology which turned the life of a farmer's wife into the life of a human being.

But it was in the fall when, over the deafening noise of harvester or combine, the cacophony of tractors and wagons bringing in and unloading the last loads of corn, we looked at each other, Daniel and I, and Kenny, and Rob and Tim. Then, we threw our hats up in the air and caught them again in the ancient gesture of graduands on graduation day. The last load had come home, the battle had been won, and we wanted no more. Exhausted beyond endurance, we would be broke till Christmas, but as soon as the land was plowed in neat long furrows, and the snow covered the fields, we would start planning again for the year to come.

Mostly, the farm kept growing. The twelve cows with which we had started a decade ago became an eighty-cow herd. Ten cans of milk taken to the creamery each day had become a steady flow of 1500 quarts going through the pipeline night and morning. Our first hundred acres of land, which had been cut up into small fields, now were 300 acres of adjoining land, all properly tilled for rotating crops. The small silo which was there when we bought the place was replaced by three towering units of 80 feet, and Daniel became agile as a squirrel climbing up and down their ladders. The small Case D tractor, so bravely bought with the last of our savings, had lost out to four tractors of various size and capacity. A neat line of modern equipment slowly and over a number of years began to fill the implement shed at the cost of thousands of dollars. In addition, large sums went into feeding and milking equipment, complete with a computer to monitor these systems. Our ability to cope with these many changes would be a key factor in our survival as farmers.

But some things never changed. There was always the worry about a sick calf or a cow in labor. There remained the concern about the weather and the crops. There still was the never-ending gamble of tying up one's livelihood in the uncertainties of the weather and markets. Farm life in general would always be well-seasoned by disappointments, even if in time these, too, lost some of their sting through sheer familiarity. Most of all, there would always be times like this, when I could just stand there, either alone or with my husband at my side, savoring that feeling of wonder, excitement, and gratitude at having been able to assist in the birth of a perfectly-formed little creature, a new life representing life in all its forms everywhere.

Never did I fail to learn the lessons taught by life on the farm. As I watched this newborn calf struggle to its feet and see it walk purposefully towards its mother's milk, I marvelled at how independent baby calves are, much more independent than human babies who are helplessly dependent on their parents for many years.

I had learned the wisdom of that lengthy dependence of humans upon each other. This newborn calf so independent from its mother now will nevertheless always remain a member of the herd. Its attachment to its familiar surroundings will persist throughout life. The metaphor, "one flock, one shepherd," may not be appropriate for human communities, but it is certainly descriptive of a herd of cows.

Human babies, on the other hand, remain dependent on their parents for years. This loving symbiosis with the primary caregivers, an attachment that appears as clinging, crying, or helpless dependence, will grow from a primitive attachment into the more advanced and sophisticated sympathy, patience and altruistic love of the adult.[11] Paradoxically, it is this secure attachment and loyalty to significant others that nurtures uniqueness and eventually allows humans to work out the long and difficult process of appreciating one's being different.

Chapter Eight
In Memory of Mary Magdalen

No one, myself included, had been able to see my friendship with John and consecutive attachments as a way of coping with the loss of meaning and of the sense of belonging that I had before coming to Canada. I had often said, somewhat jokingly, that I had a hole in my heart so big that John had fallen into it. At this Daniel had nodded, in half-puzzlement, half-understanding—it really takes one immigrant to understand another—but he had still hated it. And how he had hated it! Yet, it was this attachment to John that had taken the place of my primary ties with my family of origin. It had been a way of transferring family ties from one country to another, from one culture to another. It was a way of bonding in altruistic love, sympathy and understanding.

My self-esteem had been so tied up with my people in Belgium that as long as I could somehow remember my own parents as loving and supportive, my self-esteem allowed me to be loving and warm toward people. If, however, the rejected child in me remembered my parents as critical and narrow, I closed up, and I became hard and defensive toward everyone. Since I could not test the script of my parents' love that I carried in my memory to the real parental relationship very often, those memories could be anything that floated up to my consciousness. Whenever I returned from an affectionate encounter with my parents in Belgium, I felt whole again. But as time passed, the childhood memories with their ensuing messages of angry criticism and their threat of rejection returned. The result was that I continually sought reassurance in the experience of falling in love. Every time a new friendship came to its inevitable end, I was once again faced with the rejecting parent.

"You are nothing!" shouted my father, when he pun-
ished me for running off to my grandmother's house.

His words were really meant for his mother.
But I was the one who heard them.
He was yelling at me.
My mother said nothing.
She too wanted nothing to do with her mother-in-law,
nor with her stepmother.
To her, they were nothing but trouble.
When for long periods of time I heard little
from my father or my mother,
I felt again my father's anger,
and my mother's cold withdrawal.
Their anxious rage may have had nothing to do with
    me.
Yet many times did I believe,
that I was "nothing."
And when in turn my teenage daughter turned on
    me,
because I would not let her go to the dance,
she, too, took up the chorus and shouted,
"You are nothing."

My overinvolvement with John, among others, had not been a way to deal with marital difficulties as much as it was my way of dealing with abandonment and separation. Yet, I had no way of knowing this, at the time.

I folded the blanket neatly to make a support for my head. Then I put my hands together and put down my head between my arms on the blanket, walked my feet forward until I had my back against the wall, and with a concentration of muscle I straightened my body into a headstand. I had done this pose countless times before, a yoga exercise which helped me to concentrate and gather my wits about me. This time, however, when my feet hit the wall against which I was standing, a small framed painting came crashing down, breaking it into splinters.

I had meant to remove the picture to a safer place, to avoid its coming down someday, but now it had come down and it gave me a chance to take a good look at the small fragmented frame and its reproduction of a Rembrandt now come loose.

For a while I sat cross-legged on the floor, remembering how we, my husband and I, had bought it in an art museum in Amsterdam, on that last day of the year. The picture was a scene depicting Jesus' birth, but it was the artful combination of light and shadows which had caught my eye at the time. In it, the child Jesus was painted into a large fleck of light among the large shadows who were his mother and father.

> *Men are children of light, and out of darkness they have found their inheritance.*
>
> *Why is it that spiritual people always write for men? I wonder what spiritual women are supposed to do?*

At the Reichs Museum in Amsterdam, the original Rembrandt had hung right beside a picture of Mary Magdalen, the prostitute of the Gospels, one of her breasts exposed.

On our way out, we had found an affordable reproduction of the Rembrand's light and shadow artistry, and upon returning home I had hung it in the living room in the old house, and there it had hung all these years, a symbol of the struggle between the light and darkness that was my life.

However, I remembered much more poignantly the Mary Magdalen. Its symbolism had struck me much more deeply, even if we had refrained from buying a copy. I had felt a kinship with her greater than with the shadowy figure of Mary bent over the newborn Light. Perhaps Mary Magdalen had never learned to change the word "men" to "women" either. If she had, she would never have let anyone in her life keep her from her rightful inheritance to the Light. But then, she, too, may have been looking for this inheritance in all the wrong places. Maybe she too had played all the roles that she had been expected to play, the mother, the wife, the daughter, the lover.

Fifteen years of faithful marriage and motherhood, 15 years of devoted church attendance had left me with nothing but a gaping emptiness inside me, a desperate sadness for which there was no cure. The script of my life had been written by others, and others had decided that I had everything that I needed to be happy, but my psyche would not cooperate. I functioned mechanically, doing daily chores, organizing the children's clothes and their meals.

In spring and summer I went through the routines of planting and spraying, of haying and silo-filling. This fall I had waited and waited until it was time to go to Belgium for Christmas. In Belgium, I again went through the same routine of making sure the right presents landed with the proper relative, and the children had clean socks and clean underwear.

I had stopped feeling altogether. Just as I had learned to keep my distance from people in Canada in order not to get hurt again, I kept a safe distance from my relatives in Belgium. I felt much too fragile to risk being connected with anything or anyone only to lose it all again after a few weeks of visiting and merrymaking. In the rare moments that I was alone, overcome with inner melancholy, I clutched to the one book that I had brought with me, as if it represented my last lifeline with my lost self. The book was a biographical novel of the life of James McNeill Whistler, entitled *To seize the passing dream.* I had randomly picked it up at the airport bookshop, and there was something about the complex and tormented artist, which like this picture of Mary Magdalen, was trying to tell me something that I had not yet begun to understand.

It seemed that I had nothing to look forward to, except this trip, and now that I was here I had been through the required motions like a robot. Finally, I had found myself standing in front of Mary Magdalen.

In my powerless life I had known only one type of power, the power of being young and attractive. If I was aware that my frenetic attempts to overcome rejection by relating to potential lovers was an act of desperation, there was nothing that I could do to stop it. I could either act out in this way as a defense against more pain, or I could stay depressed. If no one perceived me as other than a function-fulfilling female, to be appreciated as someone who was sexually attractive was a big improvement.

If I had no power of personal expression or decision-making, if I had no control over my own growth and destiny as a person, at least I still had my looks and attractiveness. Fortunately, my cynicism toward life in general and to men in particular greatly balanced my desire for sexual adventures. I knew that I was allowed to listen, comfort, sympathize or even set them on fire, but what I could not do was to have a thought, an opinion, or a burning question. In short, I could not have a soul.

Upon my return from Amsterdam, I had a dream in which I was the littlest hooker. All the other hookers had beautiful rooms where men came to call on them, but my little room was at the end of the row of houses, and it was clean and simple. I was content there. With the same accuracy of Rembrand's shadows and light, the dream revealed to me myself in all my self-effacing humility. It would be some years before I would see this self-effacement and this dodging humility as the sin that it was. Some day I would learn, as Valerie Goldstein so clearly perceived, that sin for a woman is not pride, but the denial of the self that God has given, and that women such as myself deny this self by hiding under false humility. It was not until after I hung my reproduction of Rembrandt on the wall of the new house, the wall from which it now had come down with a crash, that I would begin the lengthy journey away from self-denial to the claiming of my self.

Chapter Nine

A Bridge over Troubled Water

In spite of my self-destructive efforts, my indomitable soul was part of the same irrepressible spirit living in all human flesh. I did not just believe in death and resurrection, I had lived it time and again.

That summer we were building a new house.

One day, walking along in the pasture field adjoining the new house under construction, my heart had been heavy with unnamed emotions, my mind its usual tangle of puzzling questions. The smell of dew-covered grass, and of trees waking up to the beautiful June morning, sent penetrating messages in steady wafts to my dull and pain-logged brain. Suddenly, I found myself surrounded by dozens of pairs of brown eyes and curious muzzling noses, the wondering, affectionate greetings of a dairy herd acknowledging a familiar intruder. In the silence and peace of my own piece of the cosmos, they came to pay homage to the human being who in such painful oblivion walked into their world. For a long and magic moment I stood enchanted by the glory of the morning and the undivided attention of the cow herd. Slowly, but surely, my inner strength returned, the heavy thoughts dissipating under the inflow of a persistent energy which surrounded me as steadily and surely as the amniotic fluid envelops a fetus of human and animal alike.

I had a deep awareness of the presence of God. While the new house was being built, I often sat in its unfinished rooms in the evening after the construction crew had gone. I developed a deep conviction that God was suffering with me. I felt less alone in my pain because I knew that not only had the Son of God walked here before me, he was somehow walking here with me. The question of suffering and the compassion of God was very much on my mind. This is what I read into the readings of Scripture in the little spare time that I had. This is what I looked for in books on spirituality. Not a quest for perfection, but a reaching out for God's nearness.

Fear not, I have redeemed you;
I have called you by name, you are mine.
When you pass through the waters, I will be with
* you;*
and through the rivers, they shall not overwhelm you;
When you walk through the fire
* you shall not be burned,*
And the flame shall not consume you.

Because you are honored in my eyes,
and honored, and I love you (Isaiah 43:1-2,4).

Carried by the flow of amazing grace at work in the universe and responding to the tug and pull of my Catholic tradition, I found a friend, a priest who was to become my dearest confidant and supporter for many years. He had come to the parish and had a powerful simplicity and warm hospitable personality that made me feel comfortable.

We had moved into the new house shortly before Christmas. Everything looked new and smelled new. After living in the ruins of our old house for several months, the new place seemed like the honeymoon suite of a luxury hotel. Yet, much as I experienced the new house as a token of God's amazing grace and love, material things had never had any great lure for me. Partly because I had never had any money of my own anyway, and, also, because I felt that these things could not substitute for what I really needed.

Coming up was Christmas with the annual admonitions to repentance in our Church, so my daughter and I set out one night to go to confession. As usual, I did not know what to confess. The many years of muddling through had convinced me that ethical abstractions, the shoulds and the oughts, the obligations expounded in many a sermon, had little to do with day-to-day decisions of love and caring.

Sensing that I needed more space than what the confessional could provide me, Father Steve insisted that I come to his office some day to talk out the things that were troubling me. So, the next week, once burned, twice shy, full of suppressed rage and desperation, I went to see him.

> *The person in misery is crushed. . . encircled*
> *without hope of rising by herself*
> *surrounded and knotted with obstacles*
> *and difficulties. . .*
> *no desire*
> *no hope*
> *no motivation*
> *no will to live*
> *closed off*
> *the human being is marvellous and mysterious*
> *when called for*
> *calling forth*
> *strength*
> *tenderness*
> *can surge up in her*
> *giving life*
> *and then there can be a bursting forth*
> *of quiet energy. . .*
> *capacity for creativity*
> *generosity. . . deep attention. . .concern . . . work. . . a*
> *sense of wonderment. . . some taste of infinity. . .*
> *never ceasing. . . evolving. . .deepening. . .creating. . .*
> *calling. . .*[12]

It was the poem that had prompted me to write to Jean Vanier, earlier. Jean's letter tucked securely in my wallet as a talisman, I had driven the 12 miles to Steve's office.

Father Steve could have been a cop in the Bronx, Paul Newman in Fort Apache—always too emotionally involved with those at the bottom end of society. He was a lion living in a self-imposed cage, civilized by reason of the cage and, also, because a steady stream of spectators walked by the cage each day, and because the children wanted to pet him. Still, one always had the impression that his enormous creativity was always ready to be set loose, and no cage would contain it.

One also felt that he would only grin humorously at a profanity or two. Even if I had not even begun to swear, it was nice to know that I could.

"I drove over here in such a rage, I almost killed myself," I said. I was going for honesty from the start.

He studied a pot of African violets. "I think these could use some water," he said unperturbed. His calmness did not fool me for a moment.

"No one can live in a perpetual state of conflict," I contended, my fists in my lap clenched so tightly that the nails cut into my palms.

He heard me.

"Why don't you start from the beginning," he said.

I was afraid that I would start crying, and that once started I would never stop.

"No one really *knows* me," I wailed, thinking of all the parts of myself that I could not share with anyone.

"So what you did you do wrong?" He sounded like a cop.

"You don't waste any time." I laughed, in spite of myself.

*Hidden secrets, hidden sins, the priest's mind was
   working.
When people get sick they may ask themselves, "What
   did I do wrong?"
Not so the doctor. He just tries to find out about the
   illness.
But when people become mentally or spiritually ill,
   people still say. . .
What did you do wrong?*

As if moral judgment has ever produced healing.
Perhaps that is why,
the God of Job silenced the moralists,
and even Job himself is brought down from the clouds
of theorizing and of equating good fortune with the
love of the Almighty.
Perhaps that is why, out of our senseless suffering
emerges the deep confidence that God allows us
the freedom to ask ultimate questions.

Certainly that is when
we have the opportunity
to find God's suffering joined up with ours.

Almost immediately, his tone became gentle again. "What is there that you cannot forgive yourself for?"

Exasperated now, I exclaimed, "It is for what I have done right that I cannot forgive myself."

I had had the fears and the courage of an immigrant. I had loved in the face of misunderstanding and rejection. I had cared for others with no hope of repayment. I had picked up my broken heart time and again and handed it over to be ruined some more. In the face of all adversity, I had gone out among strangers to adopt three children and loved them as my own. I had gone beyond the ethical norms of my Catholic culture, and I had walked where angels feared to tread. I had endured loneliness and abandonment by my family and the deprivation of my country of origin. I had tried to do good. I had fought to stay sane. And it had all been for nothing.

I wasn't about to be canned and dried by some do-gooder who wanted to save me from my sins. And he wasn't about to be scared away by some angry yelling. He was there because he cared, and care he would whether I wanted it or not.

I told him about how I was torn between depression and acting out to ward off being hurt again. I told him how at times I wanted to withdraw from people and relationships altogether, and other times I just wanted to lose myself in experiences of love and limerance.

Once the storm was over, the clouds parted, rays of sun broke through.

"Thank God for your ability to love," he said, finally.

I had desperately wanted a searchlight to examine the waste and debris of my life so that I could stop bumping into it at every turn. I wanted to see what it was that frightened me, kept me closed off and withdrawn. I wanted to know that there was more to me than an emotional muddle.

When I got up to leave, there suddenly had been a comforting arm wrapped around my shoulders. I flew home to my husband and I said, "I am not a nobody, I am me!"

I went back to see him time and again. And now I no longer talked about what troubled me. I simply acted it out. One time, I was all defensive anger and hostility, the next, all love and limerance.

Sometimes, I had to keep a tight control on that defensive type of violence that is characteristic of those who feel that they have been violated. I had already been burned so many times. I felt destroyed, by life, by myself, by other people, by circumstances. Too many things dear to me had been taken away. All my instincts were for destroying those forces that had destroyed me: the lack of caring, misunderstanding, indifference, and condemnation without; fear, self-destruction, self-effacement, and confusion within. If in a last ditch effort I was willing to chance one more time to have an open and loving relationship, it did not come easy.

Other times, I was all sunshine and roses. I was reading Thomas Merton. Did he like Thomas Merton? How about Jean Vanier? I was a living testimony of faith and hope.

And now I did not sound like Tammy Baker because he listened. And he heard me. He never evaluated any relationship that I had had in a purely moralistic way, but rather he pointed to the opportunities for growth. We were kindred spirits.

He also knew something about counseling practices, enough to know that people who come in for counseling feel incompetent, inadequate, and humiliated. He made a conscious effort to make me feel safe and unthreatened. He was infinitely sensitive to the pain of open and honest self-revelation. In the past, after each abortive counseling session, I had been reeling for weeks. But even that first time I went to see Steve, upon leaving his office, rather than resembling someone who had just had a tooth extracted without the help of novocaine, I walked out feeling as if all my joints had been oiled. At subsequent sessions, there was always a hug or a gentle pat on the shoulder, so that I felt that even the violent rage had been accepted and forgiven.

Consecutive sessions gave me a chance to risk, to test, to trust. I learned what it was like to have someone who was truly present for me, without fear. My husband's fears and anxieties had always kept him from being truly there for me in those parts of me that badly needed healing. He was afraid of things with which he could not cope, and what he could not cope with were what he labelled "the mysteries of human relationships." It was in this atmosphere of trust that I was able to regress and grow at the same time.

I could regress to take care of all the unfinished business, the loose ends in my Catholic legacy and my family of origin. The father-daughter element in our friendship allowed me to regress temporarily and tap into the lost or inadequate mothering of my growing years. Within the context of the history of my early leap out of culture boundness and my courageous search to define my own values and responsibilities, my need for a father figure could not be analyzed as immature regression. If it was a regression, it was one in the service of a new and strong identity.

> *I can jump to great heights, but give me a firm foothold to leap from.*
>
> *I can fly, but give me a long and smooth runway from which to take off*
>
> *I can travel great distances, but give me a base camp where I can regain my strength.*

*I can explore new and foreign territory, but let me
take some love from home.*

I can be God's arrow, but who will be the archer?

But most importantly, I was able to grow. Grow beyond my
wildest imaginings. The bursting forth of quiet energy, the
generosity, the capacity for creativity, the taste of infinity that
Jean Vanier tries to communicate in his poetry, all became a
reality for me. It was a turning point, the beginning of a new
and arduous journey.

However, it also happened that Father Steve was the pastor
of the parish that I attended. This could not help but create its
own conflict. On the plus side, I sensed that my personal struggles were taken up in the daily prayer life of the community.
On the minus side, there was the persisting gap between the
"official church teaching" and the dilemmas of daily life. There
was the persisting idealization of motherhood, the good wife in
the home, the self-sacrificing, self-effacing Christian mother.
There was Mary and there was Eve. Which one was I, the virgin or the temptress?.

There was the divorce between myself and my family in Belgium. Loyalties had worn very thin by now, and the cultural
distance between us had grown beyond proportion. While the
importance on community in the church and the continuity with
the Catholic culture powerfully attracted me, the emphasis on
family and good relationship confused me. I had only one word
for the emphasis that the Church placed on family life and family ties: shit!

Like so many people, and there are times when everyone can
identify with me, I came to believe that the bad feelings that I
had inside myself toward the family that appeared to have
abandoned me were also held toward me by everyone I met. I
believed that since my family had so often left me starving for
their love and affection, no one could possibly find me lovable.
My feelings of rejection turned into the belief that everyone condemned me.

I listened to the many sermons where Mother Teresa was praised with great eloquence, and set in contrast to the inadequacies of the ordinary folks in the Church. At times a cold shiver ran down my spine, thinking of how terrible it was to project goodness on some great and saintly figure, while remaining blind to the often superhuman struggles of those who were sitting in the pews.

It was such that in spite of my confusion about rightness and wrongness, I had retained a profound sense of my inner goodness, a goodness that was not to be defined in moralistic terms. The saint and sinner relationship between the Holy Church and its sinful members was of no help to me. This, more than anything else, brought home to me that by trying to define good and evil in moralistic terms, sight is lost of the mysterious dimensions of evil, with the result that we are blinded to the real, as yet undefined, hidden goodness in the lives of individuals. It was a fortunate turn of events that after Vatican II, many a moral theologian and priest was willing to struggle with such mysteries. I was lucky to have met up with one of those priests.

My friendship with Father Steve was to become a way back to health. It has become a truism among mental health professionals by now that *the basic thrust of the organism is onward, toward health and growth.* When people seek out relationships, they are driven by this need to become healthy and to grow. I was driven to Steve by my hunger for love and appreciation, as much as by my thirst for life and growth.

The fall previous to this, I had read the story about a girl who had become mute and deformed through severe childhood abuse. It had taken a dedicated doctor and personal friend two years of his life and several operations to liberate the woman from within the body of this mute, deformed, animal-like creature. It would take an equally dedicated friend several years of his life, and many a university course, to liberate the daughter of God who was hidden in the mute, fearful, wounded woman that I had become.

* * *

The events of my life may not have made me deformed in body, but they had given me a perception of reality which was distorted. The ephemeral quality of my few short visits to my family in Belgium, followed each time by long absences without even a letter or a phone call, the many frustrated attempts to establish new friendships in this country, the constant pattern in my marital relationship in which my husband feared my emotional needs and upsets more than he validated them, all contributed to this distortion. As far as my homesickness was concerned, Daniel could empathize with me. He himself could deny or avoid such pain by throwing himself into his work, but me he held and comforted, and he worked his butt off so that I could visit my folks on occasion.

However, as a man he had been taught that his work was to be his fulfillment and that women should be fulfilled in their homes, through husband and children. Consequently, it was my need for a self-esteem which was derived from my own talents, relationships, and activities in this country that frightened him. He stubbornly refused to listen to what he perceived to be my crazy whims.

It seems to be one of life's tricks that women are often more relationship-oriented in their younger years, while they become more goal-oriented in their middle years, just at the time when their husbands find less fulfillment in their careers and decide to become more relationship-oriented.

In order to cope with the hit-and-run relationships of my past, and my abortive attempts to be something more than a wife and mother, I had drawn up a map of reality which would avoid unbearable anxiety and give me some sense of security. Still through that miraculous process of serendipity and amazing grace, during this time I found a little book by John Powell with the title, *Fully Human and Fully Alive.* By compiling insights from many psychologists, this book was able to make me see how faulty my map of reality had become.

I saw how I had retained an immense appreciation of the goodness of God, and that I made a conscious effort to cling to what I perceived to be the good in myself. I had learned that people are untrustworthy, undependable, and that above all they had tremendous capacity to inflict hurt. To love was to be hurt, and the only way to stay away from unbearable hurt was to stay away from relationships. Intellectually, of course, I did not believe this. On the level of norms, conscious expectations and judgments, I still *acted* as if happiness and fulfillment lay in being with others, but how I *acted* and how I felt were two different stories. My ambivalent and painful emotions remained hidden out of sight so that I could remain socially and intellectually competent. Only when someone tried to get close to me were they bound to stumble on this hidden iceberg of unresolved emotions.

Very early one morning, I was walking along the beach in Fort Myers, trying to remember how I got there. The few counselling sessions that I had with Father Steve had brought to the surface so much suppressed emotions that I had become overwhelmed by them.

This is why people often commit suicide shortly after they start counselling sessions. Suddenly I was overwhelmed by the seemingly wasted life behind me, the frightening confusion facing me, and the insurmountable obstacles ahead of me.

My husband, not knowing what to do, had turned to his one solution that always worked: he had taken me to the airport. Not to Belgium this time, but to visit some friends who were spending the winter in Florida.

The Canadian winter far behind me, I began to regain some perspective, but my baggage of sadness, anger, confusion and grief had travelled with me. I had read about how cancer patients fight pain, how they try to visualize it, how they use their imaginations to fight it. Large seashells washed upon the shore became my pain. I picked them up and threw them away as far as I could hurl them. I let the cool water of the ocean wash away all anguish, fear, and guilt. I watched these painful feelings flow down and disappear into the frightening, fascinating, restless, everlasting movement of the ocean, symbolizing the power of nature, the power of God. Wrapped in a robe, I sat on the beach and let the gentle calm of the morning rejuvenate me: then, gathering up all my energies into a great surge of anger, I wrote in the sand, "To hell with you, Steve."

Refreshed and renewed, I returned from Florida. It was the week before Easter and I could not avoid running into Steve, but when I related to him my anger towards him, he was very much the priest, not the counsellor, and I lost him. He was too caught up into the saint and sinners thing and this only drove me back into a split. My split of goodness belonged to Steve and my badness was all mine. The more I idealized him in his Eastertime holiness, the deeper I retreated into a depressive, defensive stance. I reappropriated all the frustration and hatred that had been generated in all my previous relationships, and I returned to perceiving myself as bad, bad and extremely contrite.

I have always hated Christmas, and I have always hated Mother's Day, now I also hate Easter. I must be very bad indeed.

* * *

It was along this pattern of growth and regression that I was to continue my relationship with Father Steve for some years to come. Sometimes, when my conflictual self became too much for me, I would become the saint, and he would become the sinner. After all, he represented the powerful, oppressive system of the Church and I the new Catholics of today. Other times, he was the "domineering male" who projected his vulnerable side onto a weak female, while I was the emancipated woman. But we learned, and we learned, and we learned. . . !

I typed out some rules for myself on my ancient typewriter. These were brief psychological insights from some of John Powell's books. I carried these around in my wallet, but it was the modelling by Father Steve and his encouragement that helped me begin to practice these routinely.

I do not have to be loved and approved by everyone in my community, not even those who are most im-

portant to me. I cannot sacrifice my own ideals, interests and desires to buy approval and love.

I must only respond to positive criticism and ignore negative criticism.

Avoiding tasks or responsibilities is more painful and fatiguing than doing what is right and required. Avoiding problems leads to loss of self-confidence and self-respect. Hold your nose and do it!

To be upset over other people's problems and disturbances is caused by a self-destructive attitude and an over-eagerness to make the problems of others one's own. Beyond a healthy empathy for those who are suffering, one must keep one's balance and peace of mind. Do your little bit and God will do the rest.

Crippling fears must be prudently and gradually dispelled by acting against them. Keep climbing that mountain with care and confidence.

Knowing the importance of the past and its influences, interpret and evaluate those influences and reassess your vision accordingly. I must remain bigger than my problems.

Chapter Ten

Our Frail, Disordered Lives

My dear Sarah, every day all the time,
you are committing suicide. It's a greater
crime than not pleasing others,
not doing justice to yourself.[13]

That summer I began to talk about going back to college.

One day I had been standing beside my brand-new house while hanging out the clothes on the clothesline, and with tears streaming down my face I had exclaimed in utter misery: I want to study theology. My husband, not understanding what I wanted, but nevertheless deeply puzzled by my persistent unhappiness, had promised me on the spot that I could go back and continue to study if that is what I wanted.

However, now that September had come around and it was time for me to go in and register for my first college courses, Daniel resisted with all his might.

I argued and pleaded with him, but I was also simultaneously arguing and pleading with hundreds of subconscious messages which told me I had no right to want to be anything else but a wife and mother, that I had no right to have other needs but that, that dreadful things were going to happen to me if I tried to change things. In the middle of this anguished argument with Daniel, in the extremity of my strong conflicting emotions, I fell down on the kitchen floor in a near faint.

> *Typical female behavior, fainting when you don't get your own way. Mental images flashing through my overworked mind, a silver Catalina, my car a symbol of my independence being crushed by a huge airhammer, crushing, destroying every attempt for self-realization. . .*

Clear, self-destructive, internalized messages flashing through my brain. I had a long history of shaping myself into someone else's dreams, and even if I had been disappointed with the returns, there were many obstacles that stood in my way, not the least of whom being myself.

To begin with, it was still difficult for me to believe in myself. I was channelling all my energies into the farm, my husband's achievement. And farm life seemed so far removed from the halls of education. King's College was a long way off from the rural life of the uneducated immigrant farmer.

At University, I would have to be competent in a second language, since English was not my native tongue. Few people appreciate that language continues to be a barrier of sorts long after one has mastered the new language. Being able to speak English did not make it my native language, the familiar tongue of my childhood.

In addition, it may have been considered acceptable, even required, that my children would attend college, but it was not as yet okay for their immigrant parents to want to do the same. Years later, I still get baffling responses from friends and acquaintances when they look at my graduation pictures. "Why would anyone want to aspire to that," they seem to say time and again.

It was the fact that no one in my family had gone to University here or in Belgium that proved to be an unconscious impediment with which I would have to struggle. My parents had been too poor, and, although Daniel was continually learning new ways of farming and up-to-date business skills, when it came to a formal education in the Arts or Theology, he was quite content to keep that part of his education unchanged.

Moreover, I was not looking forward to spending the rest of my life arguing about pre-Vatican II and post-Vatican II theology. I, also, did not want all the evils caused by the new humanizing and the so-called "immoral" elements in the new theology placed at my feet; I had suffered enough recriminations on that account, already. It seemed to me, then, that if I was to become more educated than either my parents or my husband, I would only separate myself further from them, and most certainly, I did not want any more separation.

> *The rich get richer. The poor get poorer.*
> *Those who have confidence and living skills*
> *acquire more confidence and better skills.*
> *Those who have friends and connections,*
> *find ways and means to achieve their goals.*
> *Those who have some education,*
> *continue to get more education.*
> *But what about those who neither have friends,*
> *nor the confidence to go back to school?*

Almost 10 years before that, the fall after I had encountered my first marriage counsellor, I had enlisted in a Grade 13 English course at the local high school. The work had been hard, but my surprise at the therapeutic affect this course had on me was topped only by my amazement at my grades. I had learned most of the English language first by borrowing books from a neighbor and then, by going to the town library, but I had never dreamed that I would be able to get the required marks in a Grade 13 English course to enter University at a later date.

The following year, I took another credit, and then another. Languages had always been one of my strongholds, so I concentrated on them. There had also been courses offered in the parish where people could increase their understanding of theology and the ways of our faith. In the parish, however, I felt as if I was a member of a sort of spiritual harem. The women seemed to be there to help and please Father, and not to speak for themselves. In addition, these courses were mostly concerned with teaching the ways of the Catholic faith, and not independence of thought as we were still fledglings who were to be tightly controlled from the top.

I was no longer looking for hand-me-down beliefs and values. I had done too much of my own living for that. At the University, I would have the opportunity to learn to think independently, a chance to share ideas and opinions, and there I would also discover that, officially at least, male dominance was no longer considered acceptable. It was in the University, therefore, that I would have to learn that I had choices, and without those choices I would never be able to make the decisions that would liberate me from the ambivalence, confusion, and emotional pain that had become staple to my life.

The feminine mystique was beginning to fade in those days, even though traces of the myth persisted. Husbands were to pursue their life's ambitions—and women were supposed to encourage them in this—yet women were to make their husbands and children their only ambition. If they wanted to pursue their own ambitions, they were to expect no support or encouragement from anyone. Women could have jobs if the reason for those jobs was primarily to supplement the income of the family. Since my going back to University could not be justified in terms of my family's needs, I had no justifications for my continuing education.

According to the same myth, when individual family members, especially mothers and wives, pursue goals and cultivate talents for reasons of their own, the family suffers.

> *But my dear Sarah, it is not the family or marriage that suffers, but that peculiar kind of collusion between family members geared at keeping one another from growing. What are extolled as the virtues of marriage or of family life may be nothing more than the justification of the status quo and the fear of change and spiritual growth.*

In due course, I would be happy enough to discover that what is for the well-being of one family member, is also beneficial for every family member, but I was still dealing with questions then, and very few answers. I vaguely knew that I needed to allow myself to have my own separate thoughts, opinions and feelings, and my own unique personal friendships. However, because the expectations of my wifely role were so deeply embedded in my own consciousness, as well as the cultural conditioning of many of those around me, I remained bewildered at my own persistent unhappiness, as well as at my insistent inner urge to achieve something more.

I took to my University courses as a fish takes to water. It was an adjustment, but I felt that I belonged there.

It was also very difficult.

I had not been in school for so long that I had to read books that went back to the things that I had missed, and forward to what all this material was leading up to. Father Steve remained my most staunch supporter. He read many an essay, and whenever I became discouraged, he put me back on track.

Moreover, the College that I had chosen was a Catholic subsidiary of the larger University. If the classes were demanding, and being surrounded by students so much younger than myself seemed frightening, Mass at noon and the University chaplain helped me to keep in touch with the God who was tenderly and lovingly guiding me along.

Christmas, however, is the time when many new students quit. By this time I, too, was beginning to suffer from a sense of unreality. The intellectual demands of the course work, the emotional upheaval of having become a "working" mother and wife, and the ever present physical work on the dairy farm, resulted in an overload of concerns that put me in overdrive. Warning lights were already flashing, but since I was doing what I wanted, I paid no heed.

That following spring, on a lovely Saturday morning, my teenage daughter locked herself in her room. She was our first teenager and our only daughter. Her grades in school had begun to drop and she was torn by the thousands of painful emotions that only teenagers know. She had been alternately insufferable and contrite, obnoxious and repentant, and Daniel and I had the sensation that we were living in a real-life soap opera. Nothing in her behavior was predictable any longer. One moment she would scream obscenities at us and the next moment she humbly tried to be good. She cried out for freedom, but it was to be a freedom without any restraint.

She was our first teenager, and this was a new chapter to our life. They may have support groups for parents of teenagers now, but at that time we had no script, no precedence, and no experience.

One thing that was sure about Mary Elisabeth was that she wanted to be in control. She had always been daddy's princess. She would even become more so as her future opened up, when she would finish high school with excellent grades and go on to a university where she would shine because of her beauty, her athletic abilities, her intelligence.

My going back to school could not have come at a worse time. As the oldest of the family and the only girl, Mary Elisabeth never had to compete with anyone. Not only was she sure to be first in her daddy's heart, she would be the first to go on dates, the first to have a prom, and the first to enter University. Now this other female, her mother, was going to University ahead of her.

Things were all wrong.

My going back to school both challenged and threatened her, and her grades began slipping. If she could not be best, she could always pretend that she did not care.

I had been so busy adjusting to the extra workload of three university courses, on top of my regular work in the dairy barn and in the house, that I was not prepared to deal with the conflict that was raging in my daughter's life, and the painful adjustments that she was expected to make. Besides, I found it hard to worry about someone else's life. The way I saw it, I had never even had my own life.

As was to become a pattern, my daughter always chose my exam time as a time to act out her ambivalence. I had managed to finish my last three term papers. Having been deprived from expressing myself for so long, the papers had become lengthy and too complex for a first-year student. I was in the midst of studying for my first-year finals when she decided to swallow a number of aspirins, phone her girlfriend, and then lock herself into her room.

The girlfriend's mother phoned us. Daniel and I panicked. Mary Elisabeth came out of her room and Daniel took her to the emergency room in the hospital. This was Saturday night. Late that night we phoned Father Steve, and, since there was no answer, we tried again in the morning. Mary Elisabeth agreed to talk to him. She would not talk to us.

Meanwhile, I was feeling the kind of vulnerability and paranoia that University students experience after writing too many papers and cramming for too many exams. I had needed to come home to a safe place to recuperate. Instead, I was plunged into the emergencies of dairy farming and the crises of growing teenagers. Daniel had told me in no uncertain terms that if I wanted to study, I had to do it after all my other responsibilities were taken care of. In his own words, "after the cow is milked, she can go out to pasture."

In the morning, just before 11:00 Mass, we stopped in at Father's office, and waited in the lobby while our daughter poured out her grievances to him. In the lobby nearby, Daniel held me in his arms, the father comforting the mother. We could hear bits and pieces of the child's complaints through the paper-thin walls. I could guess the rest.

Had she not told us countless times before that her parents were only stupid immigrants who did not know how to raise teenagers? Had not other parents assumed as much. . .at least until they too had adolescents to raise, at which time they discovered that teenagers are no respecters of culture? Does not every teenager know that parents are stupid, regardless of their nationality?

Father Steve went for the bait. He pointed at his experience with immigrant parents who, like us, were poorly qualified to raise teenagers in this culture.

My mind, which had been on overload for the last three months, snapped.

> *I have adopted and loved these children in spite of opposition of my home culture as well as the immigrant ghetto.*
>
> *I have courageously paved the road for them so that in no way would they feel imprisoned by a culture that is not their own. Because their natural parents had been Canadian-born, I had never even spoken to my children in my native tongue. I had deferred to them in their uniqueness, not expecting them to be extensions of myself. I had defended them against snide remarks from nice Catholic children who had questioned their origins, and I had also protected them from their father's pre-Vatican II moral standards.*

Suddenly, I no longer cared. There no longer was anyone who would defend me. Even my best friend, Steve, had stabbed me in the back. If Daniel and I were suffering the pain of the loss of a little girl and the birth pangs of giving life to a young woman, we had to stand alone.

Maybe at the time, my daughter was confusing her doubts and fears about her natural parents with her doubts and fears about her Belgian parents; who knows? In any case, she would periodically and vehemently reject us for years to come.

On a much deeper level, however, having become disengaged from my own family, it was especially hard for me to see my daughter grow up. It was true that on the practical level I pushed her onward toward independence. I thought that total independence from family ties was a guarantee against pain. I wanted to save her the kind of pain that had created so much havoc in my life. At the same time, I again suffered the terrible pangs of abandonment when I saw how her own life and her own friends became so important to her that she ignored us altogether.

> *Other people were taking my place in her life, just as other people had taken my place in the life of my first family. Mary Elisabeth would forget all about*

me, just as my Belgian family had eventually forgotten all about me. She would join another culture in the same way that I had joined another culture, and the culture gap between us would prove to be just as unbridgeable as the one between me and my Belgian family.

I was once again torn by guilt because I had left my own parents in order to join another culture. I imagined that the terrible pain that I had experienced those first years that I was in Canada was only a reflection of the hurt that I had caused them by moving away from my parents in cultural as well as physical distance.

I had prepared for that moment when my daughter would be ready to seek her own place in life by going back to school myself. I had readied myself by working hard on my own goals and my own friendships apart from my role as mother. She misconstrued my attempts at being my own person as competition, as selfishness on my part. I, in turn, was convinced that my growing into differentiated selfhood was indeed inflicting hurt on everyone else. Thus, I had the choice of staying put and agonizing in all the familiar old ways, or I could move on and suffer in trying to find a more effective way to deal with life. It was the frying pan or the fire.

Father Steve had always dealt with me individually. He knew my family from seeing them in church, and they knew him, yet any verbal exchanges between them had remained superficial. Suddenly, the many new elements and conflicting information that were brought in by the presence of Daniel and my daughter created for him what appeared to be a hell of a stew. Something had to give. The priest's solicitude turned into acute anxiety. The result was that the day which I had faced with such courage, trust and confidence in my good Pastor turned into a disaster. Dumbfounded, I suddenly found myself diagnosed as the problemed one.

My friend the priest said to me: "The trouble with you is that you are too independent."
Later, he assured me: "I don't think you're beyond re-demption."
He was wrong. I did not know what independence was.
My daughter said triumphantly: "Father Steve is on my side!"
Later, she said to me: "The trouble with you, Mom, is that you belong in a nuthouse."
She was right.

But then, I was the one who had chosen to consult a shaman rather than a doctor.
I was the one who was stuck in a culture that believed that their priests have a direct hotline to the Holy Spirit, something ordinary stumbling mortals do not have.
I was the one who had invested my trust in someone whose superior knowledge on family life had come from a 13th-century monk.
If I had invested in the wrong bank, I was in no position to withdraw my trust. I was too busy fighting to stay sane.

I may have become a University student, but I still did not feel enough self-confidence to question the validity of the authority, wisdom, and the patriarchal structure of my Church. I still did not dare see myself as competent, as able to speak and be for myself and to take a critical stance. My role of mother and wife was all I had had so far.

She gets up in the morning, and milks the cows.
Then she goes into the house to make breakfast.
She cooks, she cleans, she sews, she entertains.
On Sunday, she goes to Church.
She prays, and she puts herself out for others.
She is humble and self-effacing.

In the spring she drives the tractor, in harvest the baler.
In the winter she pitches in at the barn.
She also takes courses at the university.
She is a good wife!
The men will praise her at the gates.
But she cannot say what she thinks or what she feels.
Because she has never learned to speak in the first person.
She has never learned to say "I."
All she knows is what she must do;
What she ought to think, what she ought to feel.
So how will she ever be able to say "I".
"I" believe, "I" understand, "I" want, "'I" need, "I" feel,
How hard it is for her to stand alone.

My religion was badly suited to my needs. My only way out would be to keep studying theology, psychology, ethics, marital and family dynamics until I could express my own thoughts, my own experiences and my own insights, in short so I could speak out of my own authority and not that of others.

After only one year of study, however, and never having had to speak for myself before, I had already managed to burn myself out. And because being diagnosed as the "identified patient" was too humiliating, the pressure to conform was too great, the loss of my little girl too painful, and the challenge towards independent thinking at the university too difficult, I gladly took the little pink pills that the doctor gave me to keep me from committing suicide.

After a few weeks of trying to tolerate what I experienced as unbearable hurt, I did what I had often done before. I wrote Father Steve a letter. In it I related a dream that I had had the previous night.

I was climbing upward onto the outside ladder of the C.N. tower, step after tedious step, holding on tightly with both hands on each rung as I painstakingly moved upward towards the top. But when I got near to the top of the tower, I saw who else but Steve, waiting, triumphantly, to push me down again, prying loose my hands which were gripping so tightly onto the ladder.

I waited several days for the letter to reach him, then I phoned anxiously, asking him if he had received it. Then he did what he often had done before, he managed to defuse an escalating emotional situation by his crazy, earthy approach.

In the months that followed, I was also able to voice my pain to a friend who was visiting from Belgium. I don't know why I was not surprised when I discovered that she had had an experience along the very same lines. She told me that when her daughter had become a victim of anorexia, a priest and psychologist had been quick to lay the blame for the daughter's problem on her, the mother. We found some comfort in the fact that both of us had experienced first-hand how classifying someone as the source of a problem may be a quick way to create order out of chaos, but that the damage done by such labelling has severe repercussions on the person so stamped. Because we both had been taught to define ourselves through our role as mother, only to have had this motherhood critically questioned by experts who had no first-hand experience in parenting, we had set ourselves up for much pain and grief. We had found ourselves reduced to a helpless rage by these incidents and we had lost all sense of control over difficult situations at a time when we needed to give leadership to our families in the worst way.

At one time, I also mentioned my dilemma to a Sister on the parish team, since the gold field of parish life had suddenly become a mine field for me. Unfortunately, I discovered that she was little concerned with helping me to regain belief in my own competence, she was merely anxious to improve her own relationships with the men in her life. They may have had women on the parish teams to promote equality between men and women, but too often these women had not as yet changed their priorities. They still defined themselves primarily in terms of the relationships with the men for whom they worked.

Just as I had often been painfully torn between wanting to go home again and embracing the freedom and opportunities of my new life in Canada, I remained afraid of the pain, ambiguity, and the complexities of a life of freedom. Instead I wanted to go back again and join those who could escape an increasingly complex and chaotic world through a church, any church which would allow them to pretend that things were simple, black and white. A church which would tell them that evil could be kept outside, and that the struggle between good and evil could be avoided by simple adherence to hand-me-down values. In the years to come, the temptation to avoid the pain of my own journey and the mystery of my own life through shortcuts or quick fixes would be all too real.

Regression. . .
Lost in symbiosis,
undifferentiated ego mass.
To be controlled
To have no identity.
Lost in another.
Fear.
Fear of freedom.
Fear of being me.
Identity
Self.
Dependence. . .Independence. . .Interdependence.

In retrospect, it seems to me that my friend and priest had been caught between the expectations of the old and the new Catholic culture, between the expectations of the traditional wifely role and the new one in the same way that I had been. He may have developed counselling skills which far exceeded those of many priests, yet he shifted back and forth in a no-man's land of conflicting demands and expectations. However, we learned, and we grew, and we hurt, and we forgave.

It happened often, this earmarking of cultural differences as the source of trouble. I was an immigrant, and cultural prejudice was too easily being used as an escape from the problem at hand. It was convenient, to blame every kind of woe on a culture gap.

I would always find it extremely painful to try to discuss my personal insights with anyone for fear of an escapist attitude which would simply blame "my culture," whatever it was conceived to be, for the issues with which I was struggling. During their teenage years, my own children were the worst perpetuators of this kind of blaming.

What I learned was that only people who have struggled with adolescent children know the pain and anxiety and grief of parenting teenagers. There exists a real gap between parents of small children and those who are raising teenagers. I also came to realize that there is more to raising teenagers than letting go, and allowing them to become independent.

As the young person struggles with the new freedom of young adulthood, he or she also experiences many bad emotions, feelings of guilt for being independent, anger for being too dependent, jealousy of younger brothers or sisters who are still mama's little boy or girl, not to mention the novel guilt about sexual feelings. These mixed feelings present in the lives of my adolescent children were fuelled by Daniel's mixed feelings about my education. Sometimes my daughter sensed his anxiety about my "leaving" and took it upon herself, and other times she keenly sensed my growing pains, and identified with those.

She used everything to her advantage.

The situation never really resolved itself until she became independent, a person in her own right, away from the intense tug and pull of her intimate family.

I hurt because I sensed that teenagers are allowed to break out of a closed family or church system where everyone is supposed to think alike, feel alike and live by the same rules. As they break away from psychological dependence on their parents, they are also allowed to question and test the traditional values of the Church. While teens are expected to do this, not so their mothers. Their mothers are supposed to accept and propagate these same hand-me-down values unquestioningly, along with a stereotypical image of motherhood. After all, if the old Catholic culture was falling apart, who else was there to blame but the women and mothers? The mothers and wives were to be the value carriers in the Catholic families. Very often, they were the ones to make sure that their families went to church, that they continued to take religious instruction. Like many other women, I too had been overfunctioning in that respect for many years. In return for my efforts, I was now blamed for the problems of my teenagers at a time that I needed nonjudgmental sympathy and support.

I grew because I met other parents who had teenagers, some of them my professors at school, and I was able to share their insights. I grew because Kelly, my best friend, listened to me with empathy and nonjudgmental sympathy whenever I needed her. And I grew because Father Steve continued to support me in my pursuit of a continuing education.

I don't know if the women's liberation movement resulted in greater emancipation for young adults also, but in our case at least, the acceptance of the teenage struggle toward independence also helped their mother in her struggle toward emancipation. In turn, my own attempt at greater autonomy also benefited the children. It was during this time, when our children refused to act as good children should, that we were forced to challenge the stereotyping that we saw perpetuated in our own lives and those of our friends and their families.

My daughter turned out not to fit any stereotype. She was not content to live through and for others, she was not willing to be obedient and submissive. Neither was she willing to fight against male domination; she was too fond of boys for that, and she enjoyed being pampered and spoiled by them. I may have been bewildered when she did not fit the stereotype of "nice" girl when she drove her motorbike down the road at the speed of a madwoman, or when she stayed out till the wee hours of the morning, but I was just as annoyed when I discovered that she did not care about the new feminist stereotype which expected her to put her studies and her career above everything else.

My newfound friends at King's College had been full of praise for the Catholic high schools in the city. This rekindled in me some hope that my daughter and I might find some common ground. She willingly decided to move to a high school close to where I was taking courses. That fall, her dad would drive her to school every Sunday night, and I would wait after my Friday classes until she was finished and bring her home.

After some initial difficulties in adjusting to her new environment in the first semester, she was back to her previous star performance as an excellent student, but her resentment of and ambivalence about my own achievements as a college student stayed with her until I graduated with a B.A., several years later.

Eight months after, still smarting from the conflict between myself, my daughter and Steve, I went to visit my parents in Belgium. I had always been able to avoid any discord with my parents during the few and far between visits to Belgium by retreating into the role of a loving, grateful, agreeable and good daughter whenever I was there. I went there to feel loved and cherished, and that was what I got. However, my doubts about the depth of acceptance that I could expect from my parents surfaced as soon as I came back to Canada.

"You wanted to see me," Steve said, "It must be important."

It was important to me. I would not have gone to see him if it hadn't been of critical importance. I was listening to my gut, and gut was what he was going to hear. Still, I hesitated for awhile, then literally pulling my hair out, I moaned: "I think that 'you' condemn me."

It was a cry from the heart. It surprised him.

"I admire you. I envy you your freedom. But I don't condemn you," he said, somewhat baffled.

Affirmation had come. Not from my parents, but from a friend. Once again, I had to put myself on the line to get it.

Nevertheless, it was the reassurance that I needed. It gave me bread for the journey. It helped me deal with my own guilt at having left my parents in search of freedom and personal growth. I felt supported in my search for independence, and this enabled me to support the children in their quest for freedom. Rather than being the advocate of the child against the parent, Father Steve now coached me once more to accept the many differences between myself and my husband and children, so that they too were forced to define their goals apart from mine. It was a most difficult process with much resistance, but the results were well worth it.

I had come from a generation where parents, even when they were loving and sensitive, had ultimate control over their children. I was now into a generation where democracy ruled in the family, and where sensitivity to the needs and wants of the children was paramount. The outcome was that the child who was the most manipulative had the most power. Time and again, I had to tell my children that I would respect their right to choose their own values and priorities, but that they also must respect mine.

This was the challenge that I was facing. I could not have done it without the opportunity of a continued education. When my daughter got married, seven years later, I could be very proud of the independent woman that she had become.

Chapter Eleven
When Opportunity Knocks

Capacities clamor to be used, and cease their clamor only when they are well used. That is, capacities are also needs. Not only is it fun to use our capacities, but it is also necessary for growth. The unused skill or capacity or organ can become a disease center or else atrophy or disappear, thus diminishing the person.[14]

It was because of the years that I spent first at King's College in undergraduate work, then at Waterloo Lutheran Seminary and the Toronto School of Theology for a graduate degree in theology, and finally back at Waterloo for a degree in Pastoral Counselling that I was propelled to become oriented toward my own goals. Because human self-esteem is greatly defined by the love of others towards us, and because the positive and negative feedback of others always remains part of the individual's self-concept long after those important others are no longer present, I had spent most of my life being overly concerned about relationships. If my important relationships had been functioning well, I may have been less concerned about the approval or disapproval of others. Such as it was, it had become so crucial for me that people liked me and cared for me that it became an obsession which kept me imprisoned and which hindered me from pursuing my own goals. This obsession with love and approval on my part, however, had not helped me to see the love and approval that I was already getting from so many people. As long as I could assume that no one cared for me, I felt safe.

As long as I did not expect anyone to care for me, I would not be disappointed. As long as I believed that people were indifferent, I did not have to take chances by investing trust and friendship. This stance had become my working view of the world and it had helped me to avoid unbearable hurt.

This was brought to my awareness during my second year at University, when I joined a group which was meant to help students cope with stress and build self-esteem. I still thought that nobody could possibly love me; that most people had reason enough to hate me. Unfortunately, knowing this did nothing to change me immediately, but now, at least, I knew that this map of reality was no longer good enough to steer me through life.

It was difficult at first to stop being hung up on relationships. But after I stopped caring whether or not Daniel approved of what I was doing, after I no longer asked my friends and neighbors what they thought of my going back to college, I was well on my way.

It is true that there were many people who approved of what I was doing, and I think I bored them to death by my enthusiasm about a world that they did not understand.

There was my best friend, Kelly, who endlessly listened to me and sympathized with me. I had met Kelly in one of those wonderful chance encounters that are often associated with the finding of a lover, and not the finding of a friend. Small and skinny, she had a way with people and with words. With blonde hair and blue eyes, she could have been my younger sister. From day one, Kelly had decided that we were kindred spirits. With her I could talk sincerely about gut-level reactions and feelings, without any worry about whether we were saying the right thing. I unloaded on her whenever I needed to unload, and she bitched unabashedly about her problems whenever she felt that life was handing her more than she could handle.

Much as I had appreciated Kelly's friendship, however, in the beginning I had simply been counting the days until she, too, would decide she wanted nothing more to do with me. After all, wasn't that the way relationships had always turned out for me? Why would she be any different? After all, had life not proven to me time and time again that my only security lay in staying away from people and from close relationships altogether? So the very first time she gave me a spontaneous hug, I had had to control myself so as not to push her angrily away. But she had hung in there, and so had I.

We told each other things that we would tell no one else, or things that we were so hesitant to tell someone else that we tried it out on each other first to see what reaction we would get. While drinking coffee at the mall, one time, we discovered that some of the other shoppers were staring at us, trying to catch a phrase or two of our noisy exchange of confidences, with the result that we moved our "confessional" to her little kitchen where we continued our lamenting in private.

Kelly never failed in her support of me.

How many papers did I have to do yet? How many more exams? Did I find my way through that huge university library? Did I know how to use the computers? She empathized with my fears, she rejoiced in my successes. She would even be "my maid of honor," as I jokingly called it, on my graduation day.

Then there also was my neighbor Ann, who was keenly interested in what I was doing. Ann was the neighborhood mother. She was the one who remembered to bring a pie or a flower when someone was sick. She remembered the birthdays, the weddings, the anniversaries. She helped organize a welcome party when someone moved into the neighborhood, or a going-away party when someone moved out.

"So how many times a week do you have to go to school this week?"

She never failed to ask. How was the driving yesterday? Did I make it through the blizzard? Was it still foggy when I had to drive home? Were the roads icy on Friday?

Not even my fellow students at school had inquired about those arduous winter drives through sleet and snow and ice. In the undergraduate program, especially, most of them were in residence, so they did not have to commute. When they came into the classroom in the morning, only half awake, I already had a half a day's work behind me.

"It is really nice that you can do that," she said, meaning the courses that I was taking.

When I graduated she threatened that she would take my picture to the local newspaper herself to announce my graduation if I refused to do it. She was encouraging, she was interested, she was nonjudgmental.

And then there still was Father Steve. He was losing all his hair now, and he was mellowing somewhat, but that, too, goes with being a father.

"You have to expect to get confused once in awhile when you are cramming all that intellectual stuff into your head," he said. "your mind is leaping ahead of the rest of you."

He, too, never failed me again. "Carry on, my dear," he said cheeringly whenever I left his office to get back to my homework. Dropping into his office from time to time helped me to deal with my own ambivalence. He continued to back me in my goals for a college education, while encouraging me to stay sensitive to the needs of my family. Knowing this, Daniel for his part was less afraid and doubtful of what I was doing. Having acquired the habit of stopping in at Steve's office, it was also easier for me to go to a professor's office when I needed help with my course work.

There was also Ada.

Ada was a young soul entrapped in an old, defecting body. One always had the impression that she would gladly have unzipped her old body and thrown it aside so that she could enjoy life the way she wanted. She had been confined to a wheelchair for many years because of arthritis. Seeing her always made me wonder why we have to struggle so hard to learn to live life in all its fullness, only to have everything taken away on us bit by bit when we grow old.

She loved me, and I loved her back.

Because she lived in a nursing home close to the university, I could go and visit her from time to time. Visiting her in the home helped me escape the headiness of academic knowledge for a while and touch base with the real world of old age, sickness and human limitations.

Nearing 80 now, she was still interested and interesting. Though she was forced to spend her life among Alzheimer patients and old people with various degrees of disability, she was always busy and keenly interested in politics and public events. She was a practical joker with a wonderful sense of humor. Beside the picture of the latest Liberal leader hung Mister April, or May or June, unabashed in all his muscular masculinity, looking down from the wall of her cluttered little room while we shared the stories of her latest pranks, her jokes, and her letters to the editor. From wealthy Protestant stock, she was keenly interested in Catholic traditions and culture. It seemed ironic to me that as I gravitated toward that culture which had sprung from the Reformation, people like her held warm regards for my own Catholic culture.

Last but not least, there was Donna, a fellow student at the university. A few years older than myself, she had already left the height of her beauty behind her so that it took me a little longer to discover the attractiveness underneath her ordinary appearance.

"Do you know where the cafeteria is around here?" she had asked one morning after class. It had already been a couple months since the new school year had started.

"Sure, it is right behind that door over there," I said, surprised at the fact that she had never joined the others there at breaktime.

She, too, had just started to take courses at the same university, but she spent most of her time on what was the main campus. Once she had discovered the King's cafeteria, she sat waiting there for me every school morning half an hour before class with a cup of coffee and a wonderful dose of humor. It was there that we took the time to share our fears and our successes.

"After what I said in class yesterday, I went home and had an anxiety attack," she confided one day.

"I am sure if we keep taking part in the discussions, our anxiety will grow less as we go on," I said encouragingly.

In turn, she introduced me to the ins and outs of the main campus. She steered me toward the library computers, she showed me the way through campus offices and university red tape. I could not have fared better if I had a husband who was able to assist me through my many years on Western's campus. Donna turned out to be as practical and organized as I was confused and absent-minded. She was also incredibly healthy. Some days, I had P.M.S. so bad that I did not know where I was or who I was. On those days, she helped me keep my focus.

Like me, she was straightforward, overly honest, and not used to speaking out before 50 other students who were half her age. I thought it funny that when she had volunteered an opinion in a class discussion for the first time, she too had thought that her voice sounded like a thunderbolt in the silence of the classroom.

We reassured one another. We told each other how well we had done, that we were doing better all the time. While we cheered each other on, we also kept the other from retreating into the safety of silence. For years in my discussions with Father Steve, I had persevered even when I had often dreaded it as a fate worse than death. It had taught me that the only way to overcome fear was to go on in spite of fear.

At times we blundered, of course. When I blundered, it was especially nice to have someone with whom to share my blunders. I explained to her how I was giving myself marks for personal growth. Did I know when to keep quiet? Did I dare to speak my piece, even when I had to wait painstakingly for my turn? Did I still need to cling so painfully to what I wanted to say that I was oblivious to what the others were saying? Did I say something serious in a humorous way, or did I say something just in order to get a laugh? Did I stay away from discussing subjects like divorce, abortion, pornography, women's oppression because these subjects were too painful and loaded with ambiguity for me to discuss? Was I threatened when someone disagreed with me? Was I overly dependent on the approval of the professor? Was I envious of those students who sat quietly through class and never stuck out their necks?

I also marked myself on personal growth in the writing of papers. Even if we made it a point never to discuss our marks with each other, we knew that most of the time neither one of us had trouble getting A's. But greater than any anxiety about getting good marks from my professors was my personal concern that my papers would reflect my values, opinions and critical judgements. I was no longer a teenager, fresh out of high-school. I had lived a life of pain and struggle. If, on occasion, I was forced to write a paper to cater to the bias of the professor, I hated myself for it. Even though I was fearful by nature, I was not prepared to be a coward in my academic achievements. I was convinced that it was my fearless open-mindedness more than anything else that helped me through University. I had learned early how relative cultures are, how limited our little corner of truth. I had learned that if one tries to preserve one's culture over and against another, the weaknesses of that culture will be perpetuated as much as its strengths.

I knew that openness to other ideas could never be the destroyer of culture, but rather it helped with the process of refining, adapting, and understanding one's own culture. Often, it is only by moving into another culture that one gets a bird's eye view of one's own culture with its wisdom and its bias. This was brought home to me even more when at a later date I entered the Lutheran "culture" at the Lutheran seminary. It is through the eyes of those who were raised in a different religion or culture that one is able to gain a deeper appreciation of one's own culture, its strengths as well as its deficiencies. But most of all, perhaps, I was aware that in our shrinking world it was through our openness to other cultures, other ways of life and ways of faith that we would survive as a planet.

Even though we were not yet studying theology, one of the reasons that Donna befriended me was that I was an immigrant and foreign to her culture, and she was Protestant and in some ways foreign to the predominantly Catholic college where she took courses with me, apart from those that she took on Main campus. Because she had been an elementary school teacher at one time, Donna took great pains in helping me with my English, especially with the way I pronounced college dictionary-type words. I tended to put emphasis on the wrong syllable, with the result that the words came out all wrong. It did not surprise me when, eventually, she decided to specialize in teaching English as a second language to immigrants.

Even if Donna had registered at the Main campus, the larger part of the University, she loved it at King's College which was proud of its Christian values. Donna was proud of her Church, but keenly interested in mine. When we were taking courses in ethics together, we compared notes between the ethics of her Protestant background and my Catholic one. Deep in conversation, we spent many a coffee hour at her house, which was within walking distance of the university.

There were many young boys from the nearby Catholic seminary who attended some of the required classes, and I am certain that they had no idea of the subjects for discussion that these "motherly" women shared during their lunch breaks. I thought then that Donna and I were the only people in the world who could discuss religion and ethics and use gut-level language with the same gusto.

Needless to say, I felt more confident with my non-Catholic profs than with the Catholic ones. I was still terrified of the power of the Catholic Church. My first years in Canada had given me so much hope for independence and freedom that while I longed for what the Church had to offer, the security that I longed for, the sense of belonging, I feared even more the destructive pedagogy that I had experienced in my early childhood when all our thoughts and actions had been rigidly censored and controlled by the nuns and priest who taught the faith. Fortunately, some of my Catholic profs turned out to be my best educators.

My first Catholic prof, who taught philosophy, was a very independent thinker. His name was Dr. Roberts, and he was extremely good-looking, even if a little on the bald side. Silvery smooth hair lined his skull and his wistful, knowing smile was ever ready to surface from under the black bushy eyebrows. He spoke so softly that people were always straining to hear him. He was such an effective lecturer that sometimes he had us all mesmerized to the point of thralldom. Not unlike Father Steve, he had the executive's respect of what was corporate, school, or church policy. But being a college professor, he had the freedom of the university setting as a forum for his insights. As he tentatively threaded his way through traditional Catholic thought, he never abdicated his own knowledge and insights for the sake of conformity.

This more than anything encouraged me to go on with my studies. If I had started off by taking courses at the Catholic seminary where priests were being trained in the propagation of the Catholic faith, without too much regard for individual insights, I would probably have quit after the first year. Since I took great care to be open-minded to everything that the academic enterprise had to offer, I expected professors to do the same. I thought it rather useless to have a library full of books by every great scholar, if many of these philosophers and theologians were to be rejected offhand, and students were not allowed to give these a critical but sympathetic reading.

It was through Dr. Roberts' openness and freedom, his wisdom and gentleness, that I learned to speak out in class and thus hone my own opinions. He challenged all of his students to take part in class discussions. What did they think about the thought of St. Augustine? About that of Thomas Aquinas, or Descartes, or Wittengenstein, or Hume, or Kant? He contested the hand-me-down values of the students. Knowing that they had only recently graduated from high school, he wanted them to learn to question their own opinions, their own beliefs, their own values. When one of the older students smugly reported that he was familiar with Catholic thought because he had been a Catholic all his life, Dr. Roberts probingly remarked that this did not amount to anything if that meant that he hadn't learned to think for himself. It was because of Dr. Roberts that philosophy was to become my number-one interest.

At first, I stayed away from theology courses as much as possible. I felt they could only bring me more pain and ambivalence. Apart from one introductory course in Roman Catholic theology and one in Moral theology, I chose mostly courses in philosophy, languages and psychology. Because of the many difficulties I experienced at home, my second year was the most difficult one. Then, I started to take summer courses and these really helped me to feel at home in my life as a student.

In my second summer as a student, Dr. Roberts was teaching a course on the theology of marriage. I had every intention of not taking this course since I felt I had been sufficiently indoctrinated in the sanctity of marriage and I was not interested in any more abstract ideals. However, this course was so famous among students that they came from all over campus, from every denomination and from various lifestyles. It was not only that Dr. Roberts had read more than anyone on the subject of marriage, but he had such a gentle, soft-spoken, almost humble attitude toward the students that he immediately won their trust. His attitude was radically different from that of the arrogant, dogmatic religious indoctrination on the sanctity of marriage with which I had grown up. There were discussions scheduled in this course on "living together," on "open" marriage, on divorce, on abortion, on homosexuality, on the sacramentality of marriage. Weather permitting, some of these gatherings took place outside on the college grounds, others in the backyard of the professor's house. Again, it was the openness and freedom with which students were encouraged to share their views which made this class an experience of personal growth.

The next summer course that I took was a course in public speaking. I used these classes as a testing ground to shape and develop my increasingly secure values and views. The academic requirements of this course were not very high, but again it was the practice of hearing myself speak of my own experiences, my own values, my own insights in front of 25 fellow students that was most helpful.

It was then that I realized to what extent I was beginning to put into order the conflictual feelings within myself. I had never been able to discuss my marriage or my children with anyone. When I had tried to take part in the lively discussions with the students between classes, my voice still sounded strange and unreal so that I was tempted to retreat into painful silence. Outside Father's Steve's office, where the intelligent and insightful me was still doing battle with the distrustful, destructive, defensive side of me, more often than not I still preferred to withdraw in mute silence, but Dr. Roberts' respectful attitude, his warm sympathy, his mirth at my blundering honesty, and his genuine respect for my insights lured me onwards and forwards. Since many years of living had given me insights that no course could teach me, what I needed to learn most was a language in which to name for myself the things that the lessons of life had taught.

Unmistakenly, a new side of myself was beginning to take charge.

I was learning how to speak again.

Chapter Twelve
Face in the Mirror

We were sitting on the patio of a small café in Ipres, and Sofie had ordered coffee with crêpes suzette flambées.

It was September, and I had landed in Belgium in an attempt to escape one of my many and lasting battles with my teenage daughter and her father.

I still found it hard to take charge of my own life, to make my own decisions, to speak up for myself, and even though I was dealing much more competently with difficult situations now, I still felt a wave of guilt and insecurity in the wake of each battle.

"I was falling apart emotionally," I said, "but strangely, now that I am here, I feel fine."

I was fine in a way. I was no longer becoming unglued, but Belgium had become a foreign country, too, for me and I felt awkward. My jet lag and culture shock never really wore off until I got back to Canada. I also felt inept because all I had now was my outdated bad Flemish, and the few dollars which always somehow managed to devaluate outrageously as soon I entered my country of birth.

Only recently divorced, Sofie was more beautiful than ever.

She was making an effort to be interested in my problems, but I was her big sister, and she needed to talk to me.

"I was eleven years old," she said, "when he forced me to go to bed with him." "He" was my grandfather, a pedophile.

I had remembered the rumors, but on my rare visits to my folks I had been so loyal to the rest of the family; this meant, of course, that I was to deny those rumors, not believe them.

I believed Sofie now.

I hadn't had a good night's sleep since I landed, and I knew I wasn't going to get any sleep again tonight.

"How I wish now I could have told our mother about grandpa," she said, "but I wanted to protect her at all cost, so I got married instead. It didn't solve anything, though," she added with a wistful smile.

And how I wish I had been there for you, so that you could have confided in me. Would I have believed you?

Or would I have buckled under to the pressure of the family, and joined them in their game of denial?

"So when your marriage became destructive, you stayed because, again, you had to protect Mom?"

I knew how my mother felt about divorce.

I knew so much of what she was telling me already, but I had never heard it from her. All my news came through "the family." And such as it was, it had always been colored by judgments, prejudices and taken-for-granted opinions.

I had heard how my youngest sister Dita had grown tired of living in an apartment by herself. How she had moved in with Sofie and her husband.

I remembered how Dita had taken over the children. I also suspected that my youngest sister had been having an affair with Sofie's husband right under her nose. Afraid to let anyone know the sorry state that her marriage was in, Sofie had become sad, withdrawn, and depressed.

And she had continued to live in hell.

"One day, I had a dream that I was sitting in a bathtub full of dirty water," she continued calmly, "and I knew then that the only way I would come clean was by getting out of the marriage."

When she had left her husband and her three children, she had no money, no skills, no self-confidence, and no place to go.

"There was the wondrous, miraculous grace of the cosmos to support me," she smiled. Her face had that peaceful and knowing look that could have been my own. I grinned, knowingly, as I thought about the miracle of serendipity that had brought me here today.

A few days ago, I had phoned a travel agency, because my problems at home had overwhelmed me. Two hours later, I had been on my way to the airport where I had managed to push my expired passport through the hands of airport officials in Toronto and London, England, and now, here I was, sitting with my sister who needed her sister.

Jet lag, culture shock, Canadian dollars and poor vocabulary notwithstanding, I was looking in a mirror. Here, in this great and lonely world, there was a woman who not only resembled me in looks and in character, but whose life's struggles echoed my own.

Courageously, she went on with her story. "I found a wonderful therapist, and I fell in love with him."

I knew all too well what she was talking about. It could have been me speaking rather than her.

"I know the feeling," I empathized.

"He said he didn't want to go to bed with me, he said it would destroy me," she said.

We touched base again. Had I not had first-hand experience of the therapeutic value of being in love?

After all, the gods had smiled favorably on me. More than once.

I could not help thinking how impoverished my life would have been without John, or without Steve, for that matter.

I don't know what would have happened if I would have had to interrupt violently an intense and healing friendship because of powerful sexual attractions. And I remembered too well how it had been the rectitude of these men, as much as their love, that had given me great solace and restored my faith in humanity. I only wished there were more people who were willing to risk such extensive involvement.

I also hoped that there would be more professionals like Sofie's therapist who were willing to help people negotiate the immense discipline involved in therapeutic relationships where, in the presence of intimate emotional involvement, there are enormous pressures to consummate sexual attractions.

> *Because of the necessarily loving and intimate nature of the psychotherapeutic relationship, it is inevitable that both patients and therapist routinely develop strong or extremely strong sexual attractions to each other.*[15]

> *I had been reading Scott Peck's book,* The Road Less Travelled, *during that long agonizing trip without a passport.*
>
> *That same amazing grace at work again. An American and a European therapist struggling with the same questions. A Canadian and a Belgian sister searching for the answers.*

"How could anyone help but fall in love with you," I ventured, smiling fondly now at my lovely sister.

And I was not thinking of her physical beauty, either.

It had now been less than two years since she walked out on her husband, since she had been forced to set an ultimatum that he make a decision between her and his mistress, our youngest sister. When he chose the sister, she had walked away from him and her children, feeling suicidal, abandoned and destroyed.

Now, in the timespan two years, she had worked through the devastation in her life with an honesty and determination that would make many people wince. She had been working dauntlessly with the therapist toward her own mental health and spiritual growth. She had been heroic in her vulnerability and honesty in her relationship with him.

She had been a worm.

Now she had become a beautiful butterfly.

She was me, I was her.

Later we walked over to the city's beautiful old cathedral. It was empty and cool and quiet. We sat in silence for a while, thinking of the amazing grace that had sustained our lives so far, and the oppressive power still at work in our Catholic heritage. If I hadn't learned to question the validity of its authority and wisdom through my theological studies, I would not have been able to comfort Sofie now.

We continued our conversation in whispers. "Therapists are now our priests of today," she said.

I nodded, pensively.

All I knew was that my sister had been ill and now she was well again. I also knew she could never have been made well in the much-too-narrow context of her religion. The map of reality provided by her Church had not even begun to provide guidance for the many challenges of her life. Nor of mine.

And if God was raising up stones to be Her voice to the confused and the oppressed, I was not about to argue.

Outside again, we talked of letting go of the therapist, of cherishing his love and warmth and living skills. We spoke of gratitude for the chance to regress and to deal with the rejection and pain. We laughed at the jealousy and insecurity that we had felt when the time had come to terminate counselling sessions and create some distance between ourselves and the counsellor.

I told her about my similar experiences in my counselling with Father Steve. "He is not a trained therapist," I said, "but he is a genuinely loving human being."

"A relationship between doctor and patient may succeed because of medical expertise only," I said, "but in counselling it is the love and the degree of commitment in the relationship that has the therapeutic value."

I sounded wise, but what the hell, I knew what I was talking about. I had experienced it all for myself.

How did we, Sofie and I, withstand the series of traumas which should have made us severely neurotic or schizoid? How were we led to meet certain people at chance encounters, people who would slowly and painstakingly help us restore our faith in ourselves and in humankind? And how did we accomplish this without a map and without a passport?

The fact that I had come here without a valid passport had taken on symbolic meaning.

Anyone who may have known us at one point in our lives would have predicted our future as very bleak, with prospects only of sinking deeper into a morass of despair and apathy. Indeed, I had despaired of Sofie, while speaking to her across the miles of ocean, the meter running up phone bills of hundreds of dollars. I had been sure then that no one would be able to help her. Instead, we had continued to function with a mental strength which was astonishing even to ourselves. With all the controls showing the tank of our resources to be empty, with every temperature gauge pointing to the red, with every gasket ready to blow, we had somehow still managed to remain airborne.

If I was to attribute my fortitude throughout to anything that I had done, or anything that someone else had done, I would be telling a story of cause and effect. However, there were no causes and no effects that could explain the truly amazing quality by which I withstood and eventually overcame the many obstacles to putting together a life of many pieces of which none of them fit.[16]

The same was true for Sofie.

We could only acknowledge the mysterious, amazing, merciful and persistent Power of Love which at times travelled before us, at other times carried us, but at all times, unknown to us, surrounded us with its Presence.

All along I had known that it was there.
Often I had despaired of it.
Sofie had named it the nurturing Cosmos.
Martin Buber had called it
the mystery in which we live.
Karl Rahner's name for it was "Universal grace."
But only one person in history had dared to name it,
the unconditional love of God,
the gracious immanence of the Kingdom.
It was by thus naming it
that Jesus made possible for all
a totally new orientation
of freedom and hope and love.

* * *

Sofie set me to thinking about my own difficult relationship with Mom, about all the things that were felt but never spoken, about the growing gap between us.

Once, several years ago now, I had been called home because my Dad was in the hospital in critical condition.

When I woke up that first morning of my visit, I had known that I was home. Not home in Canada, but home, the subject of E.T.'s longing and pain, home, the place where I had come from, home, the place where my gut called me from time to time.

I had turned on my side to see the clock on the nightstand; it was only eight o'clock. A quick calculation told me that in Canada it was only two o'clock in the morning.

I could hear the birds twitter by the window outside. It had been early April, but spring was already in full swing and the birds were celebrating. I still loved this place. The old house had been replaced by a new one, and my brother had done a great job on the landscaping all around it. There was a pond, complete with ducks, there were paths for walking, little bridges across tiny streams, benches, and even a little summer house among the shrubs. A quick walk the night before had revealed that the tulips and daffodils were in full bloom. When I had left Toronto the day before, it had been snowing, and spring had been nothing but a longing sigh for many people. The sudden sight of magnolia trees in all their flowering splendor had made me think that I had died and gone to heaven. No wonder this place had never lost its magnetism for me.

But then I remembered the tragedy that had brought me here. One month before, I had learned that my father had been seriously injured in a car accident, and was in hospital. Finally, no longer able to bear the uncertainty of not knowing whether or not my father was dying, I had thrown a few things in an overnight bag, and boarded a plane to Brussels. Upon my arrival in Belgium, however, the worry about my father's condition had been suddenly eclipsed by my happiness about being there again, the country of my birth. This had created for me terribly mixed feelings, the joy about being back home mixed with the knowledge of my father's tragic condition.

This is a confusion that every immigrant experiences, at some time or other. Death or tragedy may have been the reason that I was brought back to my family, but too often, the sadness and concern that prompted me to come was compounded with the overriding happiness of being home again. My relatives were always puzzled by this attitude, and it never failed to make me feel like a phony. The joy of being reunited inevitably interfered with the emotions that I was supposed to feel when death or illness struck. It seemed that I could no longer conjure up the appropriate emotions, nor could I participate in conversation with the other members of "the clan." I was an alien in spite of the deep affection with which they continued to regard me. This was one of the reasons that I had not attended my brother's funeral, after he had suddenly collapsed with a heart failure several years earlier. It had seemed to me, then, that family events which often brought other families closer together merely served to estrange me even further from mine.

That first night, trying to get to sleep beside my estranged mother, I had gone on talking compulsively, even long after she had exhaustedly fallen asleep. When I finally fell into silence, the muscles in my face had worked painfully for a long time. Mother may have been glad that I was there, and the knowledge of my being there had helped her fall asleep more easily, but now my convulsive facial movements, the shuddering of my body betrayed a lifetime of separation from my mother.

That following morning, refreshed by several hours of sleep, my thoughts had floated back to Canada, to my husband who would soon get up and start milking the cows. Suddenly, I had become acutely conscious of my body, no longer that of a child as it had been when I had lived here so many years ago, but the body and soul of a woman now, too mature to fit into the mother-child relationship. Gone had been the little girl I remembered, the child who had lived so happily in Belgium. There had only been the woman, who had lived a life of pain and struggle, of joy and achievement in Canada, a country which must remain foreign to them, but which had become dearly a part of me.

Chapter Thirteen
Portrait of a Marriage

I tried to lift the loader on the tractor but all I got was a stream of black oil jetting out of the hydraulic hoses.

"Go to the tool shed and see if you can find me a male connector," Daniel said.

I rummaged for a while for the desired part in the pile of junk that was strewn over the workbench in what passed as our workshop. It wasn't long before Daniel joined me in my search.

"Here is something that looks like what we need," I said.

"No, that's a female, we need a male," said my husband.

"What a silly way to name connectors," I snickered.

"It's simple," Daniel joked, "you need a male connector to fit into a female one."

"And I wish you would stop talking dirty," I said, trying to keep the mirth out of my voice. "Next thing you know, they will call putting two connectors together 'fucking'."

"Mam-mee!"

Daniel was shocked. He may have had his vocabulary of Flemish four-letter words, but he had an innate disgust for English ones.

Standing behind me, Daniel brought his grease-covered hands around me. "I could show you how to make a "connection," he said, "right here and now?"

"Don't be silly," I giggled, "someone might drive up to the shed and see us!"

It had been the way in which we had worked together and shared private jokes that had kept us together all these years. For 17 years prior to my going back to University, I had been helpmate and supportive best friend in more ways than one.

Then it all seemed to have come to an end.

I wonder now if we would not have had those years if our marriage would have survived.

I had gotten married as soon as I left home and I had never had to grapple with my own identity separate from Daniel's, nor he separate from me. In courses dealing with marriage, I had now been told that, ideally, people should not get married before they have established a secure identity apart from that of their partner. I had also been informed that people should give one another space to grow. However, ideals only exist in abstractions and philosophy courses. In reality, marriage is as much a regression as it is an opportunity for growth. It is a place to recuperate from the demands of life as much as it is a place to come face-to-face with those demands.

This is particularly so in a marriage between two immigrants. The loss of identity that goes with leaving one's country, culture and family are a powerful impetus to reestablish an identity and rootedness in the symbiosis of the marital relationship. For the immigrant, loss or major changes in the one remaining intimate relationship, the marriage, may be feared as a fate worse than death.

The way Daniel dealt with the identity loss of the immigrant was by saying that he did not understand change, and that he was incapable of change and that he wanted no part of it. When I pointed out to him that he was always changing his farming methods, and adapting his chosen profession to the demands of the 21st century, he merely said that those were things that he could understand, and human development and adaptability were not among the things that he could understand. Since men are supposed to be stupid about feelings, and to be practical and concerned with things that bring in the bacon, he had a carte blanche to avoid such things.

The truth was, I was just as afraid of change as he was.

In fact, I was more afraid of change, of loss, of abandonment than Daniel was. His whole family had been a family of farmers. When they spoke over the phone, when they came to visit, they had common interests, common beliefs and common values. Daniel may have changed countries, but farmers speak the same language in any culture, and the differences in farming methods, rather than being a hindrance to communication, are often an exciting subject for conversation among farmers of any nationality.

If it hadn't been for the loss of self-esteem that had come from sublimating my personality in that of my husband, if my own interests had not lain in the field of the humanities, and if I had not been a woman and thus supposed to be concerned about human relationships, I probably would not have had any impetus to conquer my own fears.

Still, I keenly felt that by going back to school I would lose everything. One fall, I had told Father Steve that I was not going back to University.

"But you have to stick to your goals," he argued.

"Yes, but if I do I won't have anybody." I wailed, "Nobody will want to have anything to do with me anymore."

My fears were not ungrounded. Indeed, when I began to work seriously on a university degree, the bulk of the people in the community believed that I was neglecting my family in order to selfishly better myself.

In addition, my not being where I used to be and my not doing what I used to do created for Daniel an intense experience of loss.

"But he misses you," Daniel's cousin was telling me.

"So what! Everyone is oozing sympathy for poor Daniel because of his defecting wife," I retorted.

It was useless to try to talk to people.

They could empathize with Daniel. But they could not cheer me on in my struggle to take charge of my own life.

"What are you gonna do when you grow up?" they said, meaning after I finished school.

"If I had a wife like you, I would divorce you."

That was my brother-in-law.

It was also the countless men and women at my church and in my community.

"Did you not get it out of your system yet?" some of them said.

Or, "Are you trying to get the Bishop's job?"

Perhaps they feared that I was endangering the hierarchy between male and female in that I would become just as knowledgeable or more knowledgeable in matters of theology, things that many people did not bother finding out about. Even if my own husband had not been threatened, other men were. Heaven forbid that more wives might get the idea that they had aspirations beyond what their present jobs afforded them; that they, too, would want to grow. And heaven forbid also if more wives would be challenged to fill up the blanks in their lives with stories of their own.

"Why can't you be like other women? We will end up divorced, I know," Daniel said desperately.

Sometimes it was just a desperate plea, many more times it was an angry threat. Everyone knew whose "fault" it would have been if our marriage had broken up. He was hearing it from so many people.

So why didn't we? Get divorced, I mean.

It would be impossible to tell the story of our marriage in a few pages. A few dabs and strokes do not give the picture.

> *It must be remembered that old remembrances are*
> *not reasons, they are hints. They indicate the move-*
> *ment toward a goal and what obstacles had to be*
> *overcome. They show how a person becomes more in-*
> *terested in one side of life than another.*[17]

The psychologist, Alfred Adler, once pointed out that what we remember selectively from our childhood reveals our personalities. My earliest memories, and the way I construct them in my own mind, have to do with being undemanding, yet at the same time always being secure that I was taken care of: me, as a baby in the summertime, contently lying in my buggy outdoors while my mother is working in the garden, nearby. I do not cry, even though it is long past my feeding time. I know my mother is there and that is all I need to know to be content.

During my growing-up years, home always remained a safe place for me, protecting me from the dangers of the outside world; again my mother was always there, making sure that we were all safe.

I also have among my early recollections the fact that I was smart. My father was always bragging about how smart I was. The way to get his attention was to be smart. My greatest pain was that my parents could not afford to send me to University.

Balancing this need to be taken care of and cherished are my memories of being the oldest girl of a large family, and consequently, of being mama's little helper. Here I am caught between my own need to grow toward the fullness of my own life and my mother's need for help in the household.

How different these memories are from my husband's memories. For him, it is not being taking care of that is important, because being taken care of means to be pampered. His mother, he feels, never pampered any of them. Construction of his earlier memories are dominated by the need for hard work on the farm, and of his mother who worked alongside him. What spurs him on is fear of punishment. If the work was punishment, failure to do the required work also meant punishment. The threat of punishment always came from God, not from his parents. His father died young, leaving the fifteen-year-old boy, who later became my husband, as the head of the family. It was running the farm, under the most punishing of circumstances after his father died, which profoundly shaped this side of his personality. It also determined his life-time disgust toward nonmechanical, nontechnical, nonbusiness-type farming.

Just as I remember how important it was to be smart, he remembers how badly he did in Latin, how he hated school and was relieved to drop out of school when his father died. To balance this latter influence, there was the fact that he was the eldest, knew more than his little brothers and sisters, and consequently, expected to be treated as special, as the one who had superior knowledge, the one who was in charge. These memories show how early influences shaped our individual personalities and our marriage decisively at the beginning.

In spite of the many responsibilities that had been thrust upon us at an early age, neither myself nor my husband were raised to be very independent. Here, too, the Catholic culture had left its influence. Independence in thought and decision-making in all the important decisions of life in regards to sexuality, procreation, and marriage, and in regards to personal beliefs and attitudes was not encouraged in our youth. So it remained difficult for us to deal with these things independently from hand-me-down values and influences, at least for as long as our children were small. As long as our children were not yet equipped to deal with the questions, decisions, and ambiguities of the life of an adult Christian, it was up to us to introduce them to the ways of our faith.

This, too, was to bring its own difficulties. I had experienced the great renewal in the Catholic Church in my formative years, while my husband, who is seven years my senior, and busy raising his eight brothers and sisters and missed out on many of the humanizing elements of this renewal. For him there was no struggle between the old Catholic culture and the new Catholic culture. For him, it was the old culture that he remembered from his younger days, and as such he never questioned it. It had little to do with "real" life anyway. The only thing that he expected from this culture was that it remained unchanged.

Daniel needed a tie with his family of origin, and his church was supposed to be this tie. Even though his work required that he was a risk-taker, an innovator, and an adventurer, his risks, adventures and innovations were confined to his work. As far as interpersonal skills or theological or philosophical enterprises, he expected to stick to the security of an unchanging dogmatism. The more demanding his profession became in the way of trying the new and the risky, the more he expected security from a God who was to him a benevolent cop in the sky and a church which had clear-cut, black-and-white rules. Loyalty to his family of origin to him meant loyalty to the traditions of the Church.

Consequently, what we would communicate to our children was that there were indeed two Catholic cultures, one their mother's and another one their father's. They could either escape the conflict between those cultures by not dealing with them at all, or they could simply accept what they also knew by our example, the relativity of differences in culture.

These were the two very different personalities that we brought into our marriage. The many years of farming together and struggling together with homesickness, loneliness, and ill health on my part were to be the time during which we developed our commitment to each other. Having left behind all previous ties, and surrounded by the strange and often frightening new territory of our new homeland, we cared deeply about each other. We developed an interpersonal relationship that marital therapists may describe as the impotent/omnipotent mother/infant pattern in which each of us was powerful and helpless at the same time. United we stood—it was us against the world.

What held us together was our love for the country and the identity that we had lost, and the mixture of excitement and fear of the new world in which we had to find our new identity. This is probably not an unusual scenario in poor immigrant families, something many counsellors fail to appreciate. When people move into a new country, unable to speak the language, often lacking advanced education, deeply united because of their loss of homeland and ties with loved ones, the marital relationship becomes very fused. Cut off from family and friends and poorly-equipped to function in the new country which offers them such seemingly unlimited opportunities, neither one of the marital dyad can stand alone in relative personal power. This makes the couple close and very committed to one another. This closeness is often mistaken by counsellors and outsiders alike as the stereotyped domination of the male over the female.

The type of over-dependence on each other that we experienced was also extended to our over-dependence on the Church. We sought in our church some of the identity that we had lost. The need that our church filled in our lives was not the same as that of those who see their church as social club or as a place where they bring their own innovative ideas and contributions. We could only have felt that we were part of the social life of the local church if we had been living in the community long enough to have friends there. But we lived in a predominantly Protestant farming community, and our friends and neighbors did not belong to our church. Just as we feared change because we had already gone through so many changes that had threatened our very identity, so we were weary of those who used the church as a forum for change. Needless to say, this was more true for Daniel than for myself. I found the changing scenes of theology most fascinating. I could empathize with Daniel, his fears and misgivings, but I could sympathize equally with those who were anxious to incorporate the insights of social justice and human rights into the life of the church. Nevertheless, I knew that many of the people who filled the churches each Sunday were immigrants, and what many of these people were looking for was something unchanging and stable in a world which for them had been turned upside-down. It was hard enough to come into a new country, to speak a new language, adapt to a new culture, without having to belong to a church where one no longer knew which end was up.

What irked me, however, was that as much as Daniel needed to stay, I needed to move on. I could not support him in his desire to keep things unchanged, nor could he support me in my need to move forward.

To continue the story of our marriage, however, our parents had not been allowed too much freedom to speak and think independently, and as long as we were with our parents, they did not allow us that freedom, either. Before we were married we were not allowed to make many of our own decisions. Marriage afforded us the opportunity to make our own decisions, but these decisions were often made with the self-assertion of teenagers, and not with the mutual deliberation of adults. For example, Daniel would make a decision to prove to me that no one was going to tell him what to do. My way of interacting balanced out this one-sided decision-making process; when I disagreed with him, I used a strategy to get him to do what I thought was right. I told him to do the very opposite of what I thought he should do, because I knew he then would proceed to do the contrary of what I said. It is a tactic that I later used with young teenagers and it worked every time. This is only one example meant to illustrate that since both my Daniel and I never had a chance to be proper teenagers, much of the unfinished process of growing up had to be done in the earlier years of our marriage. At that time, we had to take turns at parenting one another.

Much of our early development showed in the hidden contracts that we had between us and which reflected our culture boundness. When I say "culture boundness," I refer to Western culture in general, not to the culture of my country of birth. I expected Daniel to take care of me, and I was upset when he did not. He expected me to agree with him, and he was distressed when I did not. In spite of my intellectual tolerance for doubt and ambiguity, I experienced great anxiety when there was arguing and disagreement. I expected intimate relationships to be agreeable, peaceful, contemplative, comfortable. And since we fought about everything and something else, I considered our marriage a failure. If we would have decided to divorce, however, I probably would have felt that I had to agree with and think alike to the person that I married, only to discover that love lay not in understanding and agreement only, but in being my own person and allowing the beloved to be his own person, to be different, to have his own space, and to develop at his own pace.

What turned us outward was our three adopted children. Born from Canadian parents, we were anxious not to make them into carbon copies of ourselves. We wanted them to be proud of their natural parents and their own combined Canadian-Belgian heritage. I was as eager to introduce them into the new Catholic culture as Daniel was determined to indoctrinate them in the old.

Daniel had always been fond of pointing out to me that theology had nothing to do with religion. Just as there are those who insist that farming is a way of life, not to be turned into a profitable business, so there are those who are merely concerned with religion as a way of life, a culture of habits and traditions. Such people, and Daniel was one of them, remain weary of the intellectual exercise and insights of the theologian. However, as I was equally fond of pointing out to Daniel, a farmer will only be led into stagnation and the eventual bankruptcy of his "way of life" if he does not have a keen understanding of how business works. Nor will he or she remain a farmer for long if business and profit-making is the foremost concern of their profession. In the same way, those who shy away from the demands of theology will not see their religion as having any meaning in a changing world. Nor will those who enjoy the intellectual pursuit of the theological enterprise have much influence if they cannot relate their theological insights to the needs of their particular faith and culture.

So it came to be that I spent much time being Daniel's religion teacher. If anyone could explain to him the difference between the old Catholic culture and the new, I certainly spent many aggravating hours trying to pound it into him. Whether or not I was successful is hard to say. I have no way of knowing whether I was successful as Daniel's teacher anymore than I have a way of knowing whether or not I was successful as a mother. What my family members, in their own freedom, do with what I have taught them is up to them. Often times, many years must past before we see the fruit of our labors, and even if we never see the results of what we did, it does not make the job any less valuable.

Just I expected peace and comfort in the home, and freedom in the larger sphere of intellectual thought, Daniel wanted freedom to do what he wanted in his work, because there he knew how to make choices and decisions, while it was in the fearsome world of thought, morality and human relations that he expected conformity to firm rules and regulations. It was there that he did not know how to make decisions and choices. Rather than having been equipped for an intellectual and moral world in which he would have to make up his own mind, he had always been told that it was wrong to make up one's own mind when it came to religion and morality. The church knew what was right and wrong. One did not question.

However, when I first joined discussion groups in King's College and later at Laurier, I discovered, to my surprise, that many of the young people were now anxious to adhere to the rules that I had rejected. Where my generation had been determined to free itself from the patronizing guidance of the church, the new generation had no such reactions towards church interference, since they had never been bothered by it.

This again proved to me that our solutions are always "our" solutions, and they may not be those that the younger generation are looking for, since they are already faced with a different set of problems. By this time, children in educational systems everywhere were learning how to communicate. They were no longer simply listening to their teachers. They were learning how to ask the right questions, how to formulate insights, how to speak for themselves, how to disagree with each other and with their teachers. They had already experienced a great deal of freedom and some were afraid of so much freedom. The result was that when it came to religion and theology, they were once again looking for some of the hand-me-down variety of beliefs and values.

Living one's own story is especially difficult for people within religious systems because they are rarely encouraged to do so; rather they are expected to live by hand-me-down beliefs and values. However, if you love God with all your heart, with all your mind, with

your whole being, you may come up with some origi-
nal thoughts of your own. [18]

Another example of how the solutions that we find to our
problems are ours and not necessarily someone else's was the
application of feminist values. Middle-aged women like myself
may have needed to be reminded time and again not to escape
the challenges of their individual lives by reducing their identity to that of mother and wife. Meanwhile, the young generation of women had never experienced the feminine mystique;
they took it for granted that they would have the benefits of
education and meaningful work for which their foremothers had
fought. But they also wanted all the blessings of family and
marriage, to boot. Here again, our answers would no longer fit
their questions, since their predicament was that of having too
many opportunities for self-expression, and of how to choose
among them.

Getting back to my own story, however, my problem still was
one of breaking out of the mold. Daniel had only been superfi-
cially supportive when I went back to University, because he
felt as if he was losing his place in my life. I, on the other hand,
was so excited about my new courses that I wanted to share my
happiness with him. His resentment grew and his tolerance for
my enthusiasm wore very thin. He felt that he had been my
mentor and protector for all these years and I did not appreciate it. I felt that I had supported him for all these years and
now he showed no inclination toward supporting me. As a matter of fact, if I had wanted to wait around for his support, I
would have had to wait for an awful long time.

What had been our greatest strength, our togetherness, was
also our greatest weakness. In the isolation of our marriage, I
had been carrying the bulk of Daniel's fears in order to keep
him from feeling helpless and afraid—fearful of every other relationship and of every challenge to independent thinking. As
long as he had his family and his farm to take care of, he felt
strong. As I increasingly learned to deal with life apart from
him, and later as the children would learn to face their lives
without him, Daniel had to face many of his own fears.

At first, as he lost the role of mentor and traditional husband, he turned to his role as father to compensate. He became the best father any teenager would ever have. Since I already felt guilty about not fitting in the traditional mother role, his taking over all the parenting did nothing to help me feel connected to the life I had had before I went back to school. Still I was happy that he took such an interest in the lives of the children.

There were many times, however, that he used the children to consolidate his own views and to turn them against me.

"But Mom says that we could go camping with our friends this weekend," my daughter argued.

"And I said that we must be done picking stones first," Daniel said.

"But could you please pay us tonight, Dad, because I want to get my new shoes," Mary Elisabeth was sucking up to him.

"How come Mom is not helping us with the stones," Tim complained."

"Because she is stupid!" came my husband's answer.

It was a familiar way of ending a conversation. First Daniel told them that "Mom was stupid," and then the children began to tell me, "Mom, you're so-o stupid."

I learned not to listen and to stick to my guns.

Do not relate to a bad attitude, the experts said. But the only thing that I had to relate to was a bad attitude.

The psychological violence increased as it became evident that I was not going to knuckle under.

And I wondered how much hidden violence women would have to endure in their search for their rightful inheritance.

Many years later, I was able to ask Daniel point-blank why he had spent several years of our married life calling me stupid and telling our teenage children that their Mom was stupid.

After some preliminary excuses, we came up with the conclusion that he believed, as did my own subconscious referee, that to be a family we had to think alike, feel alike and act alike. He also believed that a wife should never outshine her husband in any way. It was a man's world, and it was to stay that way.

Even that may not have had any great effect on me since I was conscious of such fears and misgivings and I was prepared to do battle with them. It was part of living in these changing times. It was the way my gentle and dedicated mother had escaped her powerless, painful, and troubled relationships with her own parentage by concentrating all her energies in, and all her power over her children that undermined me more than anything, because I was hardly even conscious of this. Never having experienced much freedom herself, my mother had tapped into the suppressive power of the old Catholic culture to consolidate her own power over her children. The effect had been that the smallest of disagreements resulted in self-righteous attacks on those who did not share her views. I had learned at an early age to stay on my mother's good side and never to disagree with her. Coming out of such a closed system, I expected to have to suffer for wanting to do my own thing.

Always, I was caught between my eagerness to sustain the children in their search for independence, and the fact that they preferred to turn to their Dad whenever they still needed to enjoy their dependence on him. However, when Tim refused to go to church, Mary Elisabeth's life resembled a soap opera, and my youngest son told us in no uncertain terms that "Catholic education sucks," it still was not easy for us to let our children make choices that went against the values that we had held for so long. Because my own differentiation process had always been riddled by pain and anxiety, my fear of confrontation and ubiquity was always ready to surface at any moment. Any inkling of discord between my children, Daniel or myself made me feel like a failure as a mother, as a wife, or as a daughter.

It was during this time in which our children began to grow independent that Daniel also needed to become more independent from all of us. In a massive attempt to preserve the status quo, I was scapegoated as the stupid one, the one who was causing our family, as it had been up until now, to fall apart.

Fortunately, by now I was well on my way to discovering that I was far from stupid.

> *It had been 15 years since I had told a marriage counsellor that I was taking the flak for the whole family by insisting on the freedom to be myself. It had been a long 15 years, and I doubt if any of my children ever appreciated it. For all I know they wanted a "traditional" mother, they certainly did not want the constant conflict that I was causing.*

In retrospect, however, I realize that our fears that our family would fall apart were very real. I had sensed very much that their scapegoating tactics toward me were caused by their father's and their own insecurity. But once having chosen to make my own goals independent of my husband's approval, I was prepared to break away from my own dependence on his approval. Without my continuing education, however, and the support of my new friends, I would not have been able to take such a stand. Now I could say, "I like," "I believe," "I don't agree," "I am going to do this," "I will not do that."[19]

It was during the parenting stage in our life that we were able to deal with the unfinished business in our own upbringing. During this period, when our children were oscillating between extremes of infantile dependence and teenage delusions of omnipotence, we as parents also had to learn to juggle our own needs for togetherness and for independence.

As for many parents, this time was for us a time of angry blaming and self-justification. Daniel created a triangle between himself, my daughter, and me. It did not make things easier.

"This is a nice restaurant. I love it here," I said.

"We should have asked Mary Elisabeth to come, she really wanted to," Daniel said emphatically

"But I thought it could be some time for us to be together, since we are always so busy."

My husband was quiet for the longest time. Then suddenly he said, "Mama would have loved all this food. She could never leave anything on her plate."

We could not go out to dinner. We could not go away for a weekend. The conversation inevitably turned to either my husband's daughter or his mother. They still had potential as "ideal women." If I had failed the test of perfect womanhood, there was still my mother-in-law and my daughter. The dream dies harder than the truth.

"You *were* a good wife," Daniel sighed, putting emphasis on the past tense. I may as well not have been there.

Then Mary Elisabeth left home to live in her own apartment. Daniel was devastated.

Shortly after, his mother died of cancer. He did not speak to me for months. When I tried to reach out to him, he pushed me coldly and angrily away. He went from denial to anger, a rage which he vented on me, until, finally, he became depressed.

The sense of loss that he had felt when I "left" him to go back to University and become my own person, a loss that he had tried to alleviate by intensifying his relationships with his daughter and his mother, had came to a head.

He had never learned to deal with loss. He also never relied on the warmth and living skills of others who could help him deal with things that he could not understand. The art of human relating to him was a bunch of baloney. If you couldn't see it, and you couldn't touch it, it wasn't there. If it wasn't his skill, it was no skill. In this he did not differ too much from most people who specialize in one thing and remain ignorant of everything else. Besides, men are supposed to be "practical" and ignorant about feelings, even of their own feelings.

His cousin was of some help, but she lived in the city and we hardly ever saw her. His relatives in Belgium, too, could be of some help, but we saw them even less.

So we did what we had always done. We muddled through.

By now, I had some insights into the grieving process. By now, I could use the things that I had learned at University to understand my own marriage. Mostly, by now, I learned that moral admonishing, the shoulds and the oughts were useless. I had also learned that forgiveness was often a matter of seeing things in a different light, that it had to do with understanding the intricate web of the human psyche.

So I waited.

When spring came, my husband decided to come back to the living.

No apologies were needed. Home is the place where, whenever you return, they have to take you back.

We still made some very good connections.

Never mind that he never liked to call it "fucking."

A card that I bought for the occasion expressed my feelings for Daniel, at the time.

> *We used to be so comfortable together,*
> *used to communicate so openly,*
> *but there is tension now that makes me*
> *want to weigh every word before I speak.*
> *I don't know what's wrong. . .*
> *I only know it hurts to feel this way,*
> *and I wish we could go back to yesterday*
> *and find each other the same people we were back*
> *then.*

But never do we go back to being the same people that we were yesterday. Like so many people we, too, had labored under the conviction that to break away from old stereotypes would be harmful to marriage and the family as we know it. This was because of the assumption that one person's advantage comes from another's pain or frustration and vice versa. As long as I had felt that I had to sacrifice my own personhood to remain in my husband's shadow, I had felt resentful. When I had moved out of that role, he had felt threatened and I had felt guilty about pursuing my own goals. As I doggedly clung to my goals and aspirations, I did find that old guilt feelings died to make room for a healthier outlook. What turned out to be good for me showed to be beneficial to the family as a whole. And once we came to the realization that personal growth and maturity in each one of us made for a happier marriage, our minds were put at ease.

In retrospect, I think that if I had to do it over again I would probably take things more slowly. It was not that I was not doing the right thing, but because of the many wasted years, I overcorrected. I was afraid to be very sensitive to the repercussions that my course work was having on the whole family. If I had been, I would most certainly have aborted my education prematurely. I had to block out my awareness of family's needs as much as my guilt feelings would allow, so as not to be tempted to retract to familiar ground.

I had gone for broke.

But then, wars are never fought under perfect circumstances.

And the war had been real. It was a battle for the right to my own personhood. Fortunately, Daniel and I had enough history together and enough commitment to each other to survive.

Chapter Fourteen
Pushing back the Boundaries

To be known, understood and respected, as well as to be successful at what one thinks to be important, are probably the two main sources of human self-esteem. In these past few years I had begun to tap into these sources. Through my counselling sessions with Steve, I had been able to reveal parts of myself that had remained hidden and unacknowledged. Then, in my years at King's College, for the first time in my life, I was able to be successful in the tasks in which I wished to succeed, the tasks of thinking and knowing logically as well as intuitively, of speaking as well as listening, of knowing the answers as well as the questions, of asserting myself as well as of being perceptive, of being adultlike as well as childlike. In short, I was beginning to succeed at the job of realizing my own potential. I was defining success on my own terms rather than having it defined by others.

I was to find a greater space in another branch of the Christian tradition, but not without undue criticism.

"But I am sincerely worried about you," said the kindly professor, who was in charge of training the next generation of priests, upon discovery of my application for admission to Waterloo Lutheran seminary. "I wish you would reconsider."

"I am 40 years old," I said. "I should be able to decide for myself what I need to do."

After having spent some time in a Roman Catholic seminary, I had decided to try my luck at the W.L.S., but I was getting some very paternal warnings from my Thomistic philosophy professor. Reformation theologians, in general, and moral theologians, in particular, were not to be trusted. Even many of the new Catholic theologians were on the wrong track and misleading the flock. How was I, an inexperienced laywoman, to find my way through such complex intellectual abstractions?

But I had felt stifled here at the Catholic seminary.

> *They had it all defined, priesthood, womanhood,*
>   *manhood*
> *They had it all neatly compartmentalized.*
> *They knew what was sin and what was virtue,*
> *What was profane and what was sacred,*
> *The holy and the unholy,*
> *The spiritual and the sensual,*
> *The rational and the emotional,*
> *They had all the blueprints, straight from the*
>   *mind of God*
> *All you had to do was chop people to the right length*
>   *to fit the proper mold.*

For so long they believed that there was this blueprint in the mind of God according to which human beings should live.

No one could deviate from that blueprint without disobeying God.

What they were not aware of was that this blueprint, for a great part at least, had been conjured up by a white Western patriarchal culture. What they were cognizant of, however, were the precepts of Vatican II, and the fact that men and women are authors of their own destiny, creators of their own fate.

God allowed human beings to develop in their own freedom and personal choice.

They had experienced a paradigm shift. In the earlier paradigm, the course of human destiny was determined by the blueprint in the mind of God. Now they were hearing that human beings must develop in their own freedom, and that this freedom was open-ended. The result was that they shifted back and forth uncomfortably between new demands and old expectations.

The theologians knew all that, of course. There had been the seminary library filled with books of some of the most brilliant men and women, both Catholic and Protestant.

There were Karl Rähner and Bernard Lonergan, Hans Küng and Edward Schillebeeckx; there were Charles Curran and Bernard Häring. There were Wolfhart Pannenberg and Jürgen Moltmann, Karl Barth and Paul Tillich. There were the French, the German, the Dutch and the American theologians. I felt great kinship with them, especially the Europeans. Genes will out, and my genes were still telling me from where I had come.

There were the men, but there were also the women. There was Rosemary Radford Reuther, Elisabeth Fiorenza, Catherina Halkes and Dorothy Soëlle. It was the women who made me realize how, by valuing ourselves only in relation to men, women had put far too little value on each other.

And they were all there, clamoring to be heard.

I felt strongly that, while the teachers at the seminary took great pride in their maintaining of a vital link between good philosophy and good theology, they arbitrarily rejected too many of the insights of contemporary philosophy when these did not seem to fit their theology. Along with these, they rejected those theologians who did incorporate those insights into their theology.

I also felt that neither God nor dogma needed to be so fiercely defended. Had not Karl Rahner said that dogma was the starting point of all our questioning? Why would anyone have to defend God or his existence? Those who believed in God's existence, and those who doubted it were looking at two sides of the same coin. I was only starting my questioning; I did not need to hear the defense of absolutist answers.

I had always loved the questions as much as the answers.

Perhaps it was because the answers never made any sense before I was burning inside with the questions.

It seemed to me that by outlawing my doubts and my questions, they were also outlawing genuine depth of faith.

I knew then that I would have to go somewhere else if I wanted to have the space to do justice to my own potential and growth, and if I wanted to read what theologians and philosophers had to say without being censored beforehand.

I had to go where I had sufficient room to judge their merit for myself, where I could relate their insights meaningfully to my own journey of doubt and faith.

Waterloo Lutheran Seminary allowed me that space. My years at W.L.S. helped me to validate my own experiences and insights, while they also allowed me to pursue my own goals without any undue pressure.

Moreover, I had become too indebted to Steve. I also needed more space away from him.

It was time to let go.

Suddenly, he represented to me all the theological rhetoric about women's role, place, destiny and sexuality.

And I wasn't imagining things either.

Because by now young priests fresh out of seminary were socking it to me in the name of God almighty.

History repeats itself.

They knew the proper stance to take toward authority.

To question authority in order to come to experience one's own potential was definitely proscribed territory.

And if authority comes from the top down, then they imagined themselves to be at the top.

Never mind that I was old enough to be their mother;

that I had spent a lifetime struggling with the freedom conferred on the daughters of God.

And I was hoping that no son of mine would ever stoop that low.

It was in confrontation with one of those priests that I met my shadow. I was well into getting my second university degree by then, but I was still jotting down many painfully internalized guilt feelings in my diary.

I should be submissive; I should pretend to be inferior; I should pretend to be dumb; I should be indecisive; I should be insecure; I should give over the direction of my life to others. I should be a nobody; I should not have goals; I should not take self seriously . . . love of self is selfishness, I should not be selfish . . .

This list of "shoulds" that I had been carrying with me illustrates how much time it takes for the hold that our upbringing has on us to come to the surface.

I thought back to the time when I was 11 years old, how the old parish priest had come in and asked us to design a banner for our confirmation class. It had turned out to be a simple picture of a dove surrounded by the names of the gifts of the spirit, wisdom, knowledge, understanding, discernment, patience, fortitude, fear of the Lord. I had known then that I wanted more than anything to possess those gifts.

Now I wondered why these people did not feel utterly ridiculous when they thought they could monopolize the Spirit of God into their institutions. Perhaps they too would have to learn that it takes more to procure family loyalty than the fearful insistence on conformity to the beliefs and practices of the group. They too would have to learn that family loyalty is first and foremost a product of the bold and loving acceptance of the uniqueness and the distinctiveness of other family members. They may even have to find out the hard way, like Daniel and I had done, that an excessive fear that the family will fall apart only hinders that very adaptability that families need in order to survive, that is to say, in order to achieve that kind of survival that is not obtained at the expense of the well-being and happiness of its members.

That Christmas, Steve gave me a book. Like many of the books that he had given me before, it tapped into the wisdom and insights of the sinners and saints of my Catholic tradition —the men and women that I called my brothers and sisters. I cried while I read it. Then I swore at myself,

"I'll be damned if I will ever let him see me cry again."

It was a phrase that thousands of women had used before me; it was an expression of anger that set me free.

For years the anger grew into a wall. But it was a wall made of ice, not of rock. It enabled me get my own wings, and when, gratefully, the wall began to melt, I was already well on my way to do my own navigating.

I knew that if I wanted to persevere, I would have to do it without the advantage of being protected or cushioned by anybody. Steve could be angry with me or disagree with me but he would always be my friend. If I wanted to endure, however, I would have to learn to tolerate doubt and anxiety, the loneliness of my own decision-making, and of my own creativity.

My immersion into the ecumenical culture that was characteristic of W.L.S was also a death and a rebirth in the same way that my coming to Canada had been a death and a rebirth.

It was a death to deeply-rooted, often unconscious prejudices against those who think differently from ourselves. But much more than that, it was death to the unquestioning, uncritical, blind loyalty to my Catholic culture. It was also the birth of genuine ecumenical friendships, and of a new sense of direction of my own faith journey.

When I had changed cultures for the first time, I had been a voiceless, bewildered immigrant. When I entered W.L.S., I was into my second university degree and I possessed the confidence of a graduate student. Away from my own Catholic culture, I felt centered somehow. I was not there to live up to anybody's expectations. I was not there to fit the mold. I could be myself.

I had come well prepared. My most recent summer course at a local Catholic college had been on the subject of "Women in the Church." We had two teenagers working on the farm for the summer, and this had freed me to spend most of my time on campus writing, studying, and attending lectures. Mennonite, Jewish, and a variety of Protestant and Catholic women had presented their views with an equal chance to be heard. These women could be mothers or grandmothers, lovers or nuns, but they were also the finest among professors, lawyers, rabbis, clerics and theologians. For weeks, the extent of male domination in the churches, and the creation of God in the image of men was hotly debated between the students in the cafeterias, on the campus lawns, and in the washrooms.

It was in those first (and for a long time, only) boardrooms for women, the ladies' rooms, that freedom of speech dominated.

I always thought it fortunate that the washroom walls at summer courses, theological schools and theological conferences had no ears. One day, one of the men had exclaimed in exasperation, "now, they are all going off to the washroom, again." Perhaps he should have appreciated that we were only trying to protect his youthful ears from some very unmotherly, gut level expressions.

Suddenly I knew why, at the Catholic seminary, I had often felt like a mulatto in the Ku Klux Klan—a truckdriver at an executive board meeting. I had been

> *bewildered by the distance, by the patronizing attitude
> of the men. But now I could be surprised at the things
> these women had in common, the anger, the resent-
> ment, the pain at not having a chance to be heard, the
> feeling of not being taken seriously, the despair at not
> having one's talents appreciated.*

We created a support group where we could sustain each
other in our journey to equality between male and female, ordained and lay. Perhaps some of us were like teenagers who, in
trying to become psychologically independent from their parents, became dependent on a group of peers. It was no longer
considered right to want to please, to need the approval of the
men. It was no longer right to accept the inequality between
women and men in the church.

> *And it was also considered foolish, if not dangerous,
> to love the men that had become priests; it was impru-
> dent to let oneself become vulnerable in friendship
> with those who had pledged their loyalty to a sexist
> institution.*

The more I learned to appreciate feminist concerns, the better I felt about being a woman. Since I had been born a woman,
it was the only thing that I had to feel good about.

It was in this frame of mind that I entered W.L.S. Where at
the Catholic seminary there had been the quiet, solemn halls,
the chapel bespeaking thousands of years of faith and culture,
here the glass-walled halls looking out over the grounds were
often bustling with activity and laughter. Open office doors be-
spoke the availability and hospitality of the staff, and the cof-
feepot in the lounge was working from five to nine. The lounge
was the designated place for arguing, kidding, bantering, joking
and listening. It was a place for communication.

The same atmosphere of laid-back hospitality and friendly
helpfulness prevailed throughout the campus of which W.L.S
was only a small part, so that many years later I could still call
it my "home away from home."

There were no "Doctors," or "Fathers" or "Misters." There were only Peter and James, Dick and Bob, Arnette and Barb, Christine and Sandra. If Peter could not help you, he called Alice, and if Alice could not answer your questions, she asked Harold. Small in size, the university's electronic communication system was matched only by the quality of communication between the staff and students. If you needed a book for an assignment, you stopped in at a professor's office to see if he had it, and if he did not have it on his own bookshelf, he or she could locate the desired book on the computer in a matter of seconds.

However, if there was little hierarchy between the degreed, or the ordained, and the students, there were inevitably those who excelled in their expertise, their commitment to their work, their maturity and wholeness. It was because of this that these men and women commanded respect and deference from the students. They were the true educators, those whose authority did not come from without, but from within. They may have appeared to be ordinary, but there was nothing ordinary about them.

* * *

I walked hurriedly along the long corridor toward the chapel for noonhour services, the sound of my high-heeled shoes on the ceramic tile echoing behind me.

A smattering of profs and students were waiting outside the chapel doors, their long white robes fluttering in the breeze. They were welcoming people to the Eucharistic celebration. Recognizing a couple of my own teachers among them, and never having been too good at separating the sacred from the profane, I genuflected jestingly before them on my way through the chapel doors. The result was roaring laughter.

"I don't think we should let Catholics in here," Peter said facetiously.

"Especially not the ones who are too eager to speak their minds," James retorted.

The laughter, of course, was only an extension of the learning and the communication that went on in the classrooms. It was prompted by our joining for prayer and sharing in the Eucharist. While the theologians were arguing about the permissibility and validity of shared Communion between Catholics and Protestants, it was our sharing of Communion that brought about the validity and permissibility.

It was this kind of wonderfully serious laughter that could support the weight of the four centuries of differences between Catholics and Protestants. It was the laughter which deflated our prejudices and fears and allowed us to be open and accepting toward one another. It helped us stand back from ourselves and look more gently at our divergences. I like to think that in some ways, great or small, it changed us.

It was Peter's turn to preach the homily. It turned out to be a magnificent discourse on hidden holiness and the hiddenness of God.

Afterward, I stopped into his office to tell him how inspiring his homily had been, but someone was already there before me: a pert 16-year-old in a pair of ragged jeans.

"Dad, can you loan me a $20?"

Only minutes ago, he had resplendently led a community of people in prayer. Now he suddenly turned into a harassed father of a sassy young adolescent. It was ridiculous, it was hilarious, it was wonderful.

The sacred securely pegged down in the profane.

My intended praise turned into jest. Pointing at the teenager who quickly tucked away the $20 bill and left, I said,

"Having one of those will teach you all there is to know about hidden holiness and the hiddenness of God."

Running his hand through his beard, he replied simply, "I know."

I turned serious again.

"It was really good, you know, your sermon."

"Thanks, I needed to hear that," came the reply.

> *And I needed to see you like this, I thought. I needed to see that heaven does not exempt us from earth, the sacred offers no escape from the profane, the light no recluse from darkness. I needed to see that one cannot find God by escaping one's humanity.*

Still, it was a bit of a culture shock. Married men doing the traditional duties of priests, women doing the tasks of priests. Ministers as husbands and fathers. I guess I had never seen so many of them together. I had never gotten to know them so intimately as when we were studying together, praying together, arguing together, laughing together. To think that only a decade ago the seminary had been for men only. Now men and women filled the classrooms in equal numbers.

I was having visions.

Even if I had not wanted to compare unfavorably the Catholic seminary, where I had spent the previous year, with this crowd, I could not help observing how much better the representation of Church and of God was when both the masculine and the feminine found expression in the liturgy.

It set my mind to thinking of all the things that were yet to be.

I wondered what would happen to the unholy split between the sacred and the profane, the rational and emotional, the masculine and feminine, the spiritual and the sensual, when the time would come that Catholic women became priests.

Sometimes, while the seminarians celebrated and prayed, I preferred to sit in the lobby and do my own homework on the history of ministry in the Christian churches. That's when I made the discovery that the men and women who had lived at the time of Jesus had only come to really understand him long after he had gone. They had remembered him, and in remembering him they had really known who he was for the first time. It was with this retrospective vision of faith that they had found different ways of keeping the memory of Jesus alive among them. The ways in which they could do this were ever more varied than the limits of any culture would allow. Just as Jesus, bound to his culture, still never failed to transcend it, they, too, had been bound by their culture, but because of him, they had always tried to go beyond it.

I was wondering what was wrong with our retrospective vision of faith, with our memory of him, that we could not remember that he had been ever so much more than any culture could contain—that he *is* so much more than any culture can accommodate.

It is through the eyes of those who were raised in a different religion or culture that one is able to gain a greater insight of one's own culture, its strengths as well as its deficiencies. Just as at the age of 18 I had a keen appreciation of the distinctive qualities of the Canadian people because I was seeing them through the eyes of a foreigner, at the age of 40 I was able to see the distinctive qualities of the Protestant culture at W.L.S. in a way that they themselves did not even see it.

However, it was a perception that went both ways. While I was forced to face my own Catholic bias and prejudice, I also gained a deeper appreciation of the men and women in my own Church who espoused the many values unique to my own Catholic culture.

Tempted as I was to compare favorably this lively, inspirational crowd to my own Catholic culture, I had come too far in my understanding of cultural limitations to kid myself that any one culture had all the aces.

Barb, my very good friend, about to become a Lutheran pastor, opened my eyes time and again and helped me see the beauty and value of my own tradition.

She had done a seminar on the Book of Wisdom.

"Gee, Barb," I complained, "you sound so-o Catholic."

"Thanks, I take that as a real compliment," she exclaimed happily, reaching out to give me a hug as she went out the door.

> *It was the beginning of a lifelong friendship. Time and again she would help me to put my life into perspective.*
>
> *Since she was "just a woman," I could be myself with her. I no longer had to cower before the authority that came "from the top down."*

Me they accused of being too Lutheran.

"You are more Lutheran than Martin Luther," my history professor said emphatically, raising his eyebrows smilingly at me as he stopped pacing the floor around the desk for a moment.

> *It was easy. Why should a Catholic woman not empathize with a reformer? Why should she not contest those who claim to speak for the whole of the Christian tradition when all any one person or group can possibly contain at one time is a tiny bit of it? Why should she not be in accord with a revolutionary who was revolutionary only because he went back to his Christian roots?*
>
> *Luther, my love, where have you been all my life?*

Most importantly, it was my immersion in the Reformation culture that taught me the value of a healthy suspicion and a critical stance toward authority. Just as my Catholic tradition had taught me the value of family and corporate loyalty, W.L.S instilled in me an appreciation for that critical impulse of the Reformers who had pointed at the need to evaluate always all our institutions and systems. I strongly felt that the patriarchal system had not taken seriously the authority of women and that women had nothing to lose and everything to gain from taking a critical stance toward the authoritarian way in which the meaning and value of their lives had been determined by men.

My time at W.L.S was a wonderful time, a crazy time. Everything was mixed up. The Lutheran dean preached the best sermon I ever heard on Mary, the mother of Jesus. My Lutheran history professor did a splendid discourse on the merits of private confession as the Catholics know it. Vatican II may appeared to have failed, ecumenism may seem to have faltered, but what 20th-century Christians were doing went far beyond the wildest imaginings of their predecessors.

"What do you think of our liturgical celebrations," Chris, the prettiest minister that I had ever seen, asked me one day.

She was referring to the curious mixture of seriousness and mirth, of solemnity and ease that marked the services at W.L.S.

I did not answer.

I did not like competition between families.

> *Did she think that Catholics had learned nothing in the last 20 years? If we had learned little else, at least we had learned how to mix solemnity with gaiety, seriousness with laughter.*

What 20-century Roman Catholics did was also going far beyond the wildest dreams of their forebears.

However, if anything, the challenges facing them were even greater.

That weekend I had gone to a conference at the boarding school where my daughter had spent most of her high school years. Adjoining the school was the convent where generations of Sisters had lived their questions and fought for the answers. Slowly but surely, Catholic teaching had been taken over by laymen and women with the result that the school was now being used for conferences and retreats.

I took the opportunity to take a walk through the beautiful grounds surrounding school and convent and reminisce about the years that I had been a mother of an adolescent daughter, years that had collided with my own studies at King's College.

It was fall. Red, gold, yellow and amber leaves were fluttering down gently from the multicolored trees, covering my path with a rustling softness. I followed the winding trail wondering where it was leading. At the end of the footpath, nestled in the side of the adjoining woods, I sighted a grotto. I sat down for awhile on the cast iron bench that some thoughtful nun must have placed on the lawn before it, and my mind was suddenly filled with pain and confusion. Too many questions, too many answers. Two cultures colliding in my brain.

By then, I was quickly becoming an expert at tolerating colliding cultures.

I gazed for a while at the familiar statue of Mary Immaculate, as she had been envisioned by Bernadette, in a white robe with a blue sash. Mary, the mother of God, symbol of motherhood, of purity, of obedience.

To my back was the river, on the opposite bank the Catholic seminary, symbol of the rational male institution with its fantasies and its dreams.

Mary,

> *Symbol of the feminine*
> *separated*
> *from the flesh and blood*
> *tangibility of real women.*
> *The mother of the Son,*
> *source of life and grace,*
> *Eve's opposite.*
> *Eve, temptress, death's originator*
> *Mary's enemy.*
> *Mary and Eve,*
> *separated.*

Life and death
virtue and vice, separated.
Heaven and earth,
Spirituality and sexuality, separated.
Woman, separated.

Motherhood, virginity, priesthood,
one on this side of the river,
one on the other,
the river in the middle.
Motherhood, priesthood, virginity,
fantasy and dream . . .
Truth's extension. . .truth's escape.
Questions. . .born of pain.
Do the dreams, the fantasies seek to extend
human reality?
Or are they prescriptions of ideals that deviate
from reality so much so
that they alienate people from their true selves?

Is celibacy
the discipline of love
or is it a stifling of the heart?
Is it institutionalized loneliness
or a vacancy reserved for God?
A vacancy to be kept
by the unmarried as well as the married,
by the mothers and the fathers?
A charism
for openness and vulnerability?

Answers born of love,
Embodiment,
the physical and the spiritual,
spirituality and sexuality sustaining one another,
deepening one another, balancing one another,
bearing one another,
like matter holds spirit,

and heaven encloses the earth.
Mary. . . Mother of God,
dwelling place for the Incarnation of God.
Men and women,
empty spaces for divine creativity.

Fall, a fraudulent glory hiding impending death,
a warning
of the coming winter
to which no one pays any heed.
Death, to the covert power of mothers,
to the overt power of men.
Death to separation,
The assurance of coming seasons,
of a distant spring,
the promise
of independent sons, independent daughters,
of men and women holding each other by the heart.

Chapter Fifteen
Home Is Where the Heart Is

I was trying to make my way to the coffee urns located across half a square mile of lobby filled with 2,000 bodies moving in all directions. The place was the Shoreham Hotel in Washington. The occasion, Women in the Church Conference. Balancing a croissant on a paper napkin while trying to navigate my way through the throng of people gathering for the conference's final address, I shouted boisterously in the direction of Mary.

"This reminds me of the 16th-century Reformation."

"You certainly get a sense of being involved with history in the making," came Mary's reply, somewhat more gentle and restrained.

Women of all ages had come to this conference, along with a fair number of men, to listen to a star-studded cast of theologians, and what they had wanted to hear was that women in theology were here to stay.

The previous night we had joined with the 2,000 other women in a liturgical ceremony in the huge ballroom of the hotel. It was a celebration of our gifts and our place in the future of the Church. A black woman had preached the homily and I had thought, "Who better than a black woman could lead a celebration of freedom in the land of Martin Luther King, Jr.?"

Still trying to get myself heard over the sea of heads, I shouted, "South Africa will never be the same again, and the Catholic Church will never be the same again." Then, more pensively, I added: "All these years they have thrown around words like 'salvation', 'redemption' and 'freedom in Christ'; at least now we can see for ourselves what it is that we need redemption from."

Mary responded by giving me a blank stare.

We may have learned to use theological jargon, but we still expected theologians to wear black suits, and we assumed that they would look notorious and eminent. We still remembered how theologians were supposed to be so far removed from earth that they could not relate to the everyday experiences that made up our lives as women. Martin Luther may have said that every Christian was to be a theologian, but we had been well trained not to aspire to the other-worldly wisdom of theologians. We certainly did not expect to find such knowledge in women. Consequently, even while we were listening to each other engaging in theology, it often appeared to us as incongruous as watching a dog talking.

Catching herself, Mary said, half in surprise, half in praise, "You do talk like a theologian."

Having finally found a coffee pot, and squirting some of the fine-smelling liquid into a styrofoam cup, I asked, "Do you suppose violence against women is going to increase as women increasingly take on positions that had been reserved for men?"

"Well, look at South Africa," Mary said acrimoniously.

Pushing all unhappy thoughts aside, I said, "We had better find our seats at the ballroom soon."

Today was a day to be happy and proud. There would be enough time for disappointment, misunderstanding, ridicule and criticism later. Now a Canadian bishop was coming in to deliver the closing address to the predominantly American conference. His subject, "Women in the Canadian Church."

We located the small group from Ontario which was seated close together toward the front of the huge room, and we sat down beside them. One of the men was the chaplain of King's College back home in Canada, the other a professor at St. Jerome's College where I had taken the course on Women in the Church. Suddenly we felt self-consciously Canadian as Remi De Roo, bishop of Vancouver, appeared.

> *The grass is always greener on the other side, and today we represented the green grass of Canada. . .*
>
> *The thoughts of green grass made me want to get home to my cows. It had been a hectic weekend, and I was glad it was drawing to a close.*

My attention shifted to the speaker. He was explaining how in Canada there had been a dialogue between the bishops and the women in the church at the Canadian Conference of Bishops. He said that Canadian men, at last, had recognized their appropriation of Church leadership and institutions.

A Canadian bishop quoting another Canadian bishop:

> *In Canada, an ever-increasing number of women are speaking out and revealing their thoughts and feelings. The dualist vision of flesh-and-spirit and the sexist prejudices resulting from it, have strongly marked their past and continue to mark their present, identifying them with "the occasion of sin." They have experienced and continue to experience alienation, marginalization, and exclusion in many forms. . .*
>
> *As for us, let us recognize the ravages of sexism, and our own male appropriation of Church institutions and numerous aspects of the Christian life. . .*[20]

What the Canadian bishop did not say, however, was what this little group from Ontario knew too well already, namely that the conclusions these bishops had reached had been the result of a confrontation between the bishops and a smattering of women representing thousands of women across Canada.

What he did not say was that the encounter between the women and the bishops had been far from peaceful, and that, at the time, quite a few nice grandmothers had been called some names that they did not care to remember.

What he did not say was that what had happened between the bishops and the women was something resembling a culture clash. For so long these men had perceived of a divinely-willed affinity between maleness and divinity, that when women theologians, historians, exegetes, and canon lawyers claimed equal access to God and the graces of God, they had been all too eager to label these women as arrogant, untheological, and heretical.[21] What he did not say was that like many a dominant culture, they had once thought that they had all the aces, and now they had come to the realization that they were not even playing with a full deck. However, he did not have to say it, he was speaking to the other half of the deck.

What he did say was that once they had learned to listen to the anger, the pain, and the frustration of Canadian women they could no longer, in all fairness, ignore it. What he did not say was that it would take them a long time to sort out what were the genuinely Christian, and what were the cultural elements in theology. As a theology student, I had been able to experience first-hand the ridicule, trivialization, and invalidation of my knowledge and experience, but then I had learned early in life how cultures make their own traditions, customs, and ideologies absolute, while they trivialize those of other cultures. It did not surprise me that as the Church opened itself up to the genuine spirituality of Indian cultures, black cultures, and foreign cultures in general, as they no longer attempted to make everyone think and talk like the white man in the name of Christianity, they would also open themselves up to the genuine spirituality of women, and they could no longer make women think and talk like men before they considered them to be worthy of being listened to.

On this day, I knew that what I had been through was not in vain, that by being open to my own experiences I had been open to the future direction of my Church.

> *When one woman puts her experience into words, an-*
> *other woman who has kept silent, afraid of what others*
> *will think, can find validation. And when the second*
> *woman says aloud, "Yes, that was my experience too,"*
> *the first woman loses some of her fear. . .Their act cre-*
> *ates new possibilities of being and living for themselves*
> *and for all women.*[22]

On the plane home, Mary and I discussed the midterm papers that we were to write for our theology courses at T.S.T.
The course work did not leave much time for out-of-town conferences. Upon our return from Washington, we would have to
burn some midnight oil in order to catch up.

Daniel had wanted me to graduate from a Catholic Theological School, so I had compromised by doing my last year of
graduate work at the Toronto School of Theology. It involved a
lot of commuting with the waste of time that this ensued.

No one could have wished for a greater variety on the menu
than what was available in the Toronto School of Theology. The
University of St. Michael's College was a reflection of the Toronto School of Theology in the same way as W.L.S had been a
mirror of Wilfrid Laurier. Because T.S.T. was a dispersion of
colleges spread out over many square miles, communication was
difficult and red tape endless. Where at Wilfrid Laurier, everyone knew everyone else, some less than others, at T.S.T. everyone seemed lost, and some were only slightly less lost than others.

Yet the ecumenism was there also. What had been happening in a small way at W.L.S was happening on a grand scale at
T.S.T. Catholics grew excited about the insights of Protestant
theology, and Protestant students of all denominations attended
courses that dealt with the foundations of systematic Catholic
theology.

At the same time, equality between men and women had
been taking shape there also. Women took it for granted that
their viewpoints would be treated with the same respect as that
of their male counterparts. Many of the men went out of their
way to reverse the age-old prejudice against women. Just as,

since Vatican II, they had learned to be open and respectful toward other denominations, other religions, other races, they now realized that they must extend this same respectful openness toward the women. "Communication on earth," Bernard Häring had said, "is something divine, an expression of the Trinity." It did not matter that the Roman Curia had tried to silence him. You could silence a theologian, but the Holy Spirit would never be silenced. Once Pope John XXIII had let Her out the open windows of the Church, She would never again return to Her jail.

The real disparities between men and women would only reveal themselves at graduation time, when these same men and women went on each to take "their places."

Before Vatican II, "We expected women to know their places," the bishop had said at the Washington conference.

> *We hadn't learned very much. All these years of education, and we no longer knew "our places."*
>
> *But then pilgrims do not have a place.*
>
> *They may know from whence they came, they may know whereto they are moving, but while they are travelling through, they have no place.*
>
> *I was hoping that I would never stop feeling this pain; that no amount of praying and hymn singing would anesthetize it out of existence. It was the only thing that would keep reminding me of everything that was out of joint in the community of Jesus Christ.*

That year Mary was my best friend through it all. We ate lunch together in Toronto and discussed our assignments. She was also a feminist. And if feminists were supposed to be loud, angry, shrill, frustrated, aggressive and men-hating, then Mary, nor any of my other feminist friends fit the stereotype. She was soft-spoken, gentle, cautious, determined, and sometimes fearful. Like me, she was also living with three men, one of them her husband, two her sons.

At least I think that I had two sons living with me.

I could tell by the trail of dirty socks from the bathroom to the laundry room. By the newspapers spread out over the dirty dinner dishes still on the table when I came home late. By the litter of shoes and sneakers on the steps.

They may have known enough to clean up behind themselves when they were children, but now that they were adult men, they could no longer be bothered by such trivial tasks.

Intellectually, Mary and I were like two peas in a pod. We agreed on theology and on feminism. We sought out conferences like the one in Washington where we could see the new face of the Church. We were both keenly interested in theological studies and we would go to any length to achieve our goal. In most of our experiences of anger and of feeling like aliens in our own Church, we were like sisters. I was grateful for her company; it emboldened me, it made me feel less lonely in my aspirations. She was fighting the same shadows as I was, the admonishing to be humble, to be self-effacing, to cower unquestioningly to authority.

We were to graduate on the same day.

That summer preceding my graduation had been the hottest summer in recorded history. Every day the mercury persisted in its steady climb. There was no escape from the heat, other than going to town to sit for awhile in an air-conditioned coffee shop, or look around in a department store.

It had been my pity for men and beasts that had kept me going.

Every afternoon, Sunday or weekday, at three o'clock I ventured out into the murderous heat to find the cows huddled in the shade, their ears and tongues hanging down in stupid exhaustion. I gently but firmly herded them back into the barn where at least there were fans blowing, mercifully skimming a couple of degrees off the top of the day.

Whenever I was herding the animals toward the barn, the flies descended on me in droves. The cows may have come equipped with their own flyswatter, but I had no such tools. Occasionally, a tail whacked me in the eyes as a cow angrily aimed at the flies. I was wishing that some of my environment conscious, back-to-nature professors were here to see me.

Back in the barn, the voice of my brother-in-law came over the two-way radio: "I have three wagons full of wheat, I need some empties."

"I have two right here," I shouted back, "I was gonna bring them to the field, but I wanted to put the cows in the barn first."

"Now, this early already?" came the surprised reply.

"It is so goddamned hot for them," I argued.

"O.K., but bring the empty wagons over to the south end of the wheat field as soon as possible."

"Your wife bring you lunch yet?" I remembered to ask.

"Nope."

"You want a ham sandwich?"

"Yup."

They, my husband and his brother, were often too tired, too hot, or too hurried to eat.

They did not even think of eating. They may have been well over 40, but they would never be fat.

I made up some sandwiches and put them in a brown paper bag with two cans of pop. Then, my eyes squinting against the sun, I climbed into the cab of the tractor which was hooked up to the grain wagons, and I turned on the air conditioner.

For a few minutes, I gave the wonderfully cold air a chance to bring my body temperature back to normal. Involuntarily, a big smile spread over my face.

The radio was blaring. It was always on full blast when there were teenagers around. "Tomorrow's forecast promises more of the same temperatures. Beachgoers in Collingwood claim that this has been the best summer ever." I turned off the radio.

I did not want to hear how people were having a good time splashing around in the lake.

Mostly, I did not want to think about air-conditioned rooms where students and professors where joining in animated intellectual battles. My life during the summer was light years removed from the halls of education.

I shifted a couple of levers and throttled the tractor to full power. The south end, did he say? When I got there, the combine was at the north end. It would take 20 minutes of waiting before the farmer, who forgot to have his lunch, together with his combine, came clamoring back to the south end. It seemed that no matter where I took their lunch, Daniel or his brother always managed to be on the opposite side of the field when I got there. No wonder my days evaporated in the space created by hundreds of acres of crops and pasture fields full of cows.

It was my pity for men and beast that kept me going, yet it was also the cool morning hours, before the sun began to scorch us all out of existence, when I took the time to work on my master's thesis.

I had read everything that I needed to take out of my studies of the last years to give theological expression to many of my life's experiences.

I knew that there was more to suffering than what was the result of evil in the world.

Suffering and pain were also the result of bearing with the limits of nature in general and of human nature in particular. When I thought back on my own life, I realized that none of the people who had caused me so much suffering had been deliberately wicked. Many of them had tried heroically to respond to the overwhelming challenges of their lives.

But they had also been up against the same human boundaries by which we are all limited. They had been limited by their culture, the confines of time and space, by the restrictions of the social or institutional structures to which they belonged, by their own needs, and by their own personal history.

It was to help people accept these limitations while fighting courageously to overcome them that Jesus had come into the world.

Jesus' life and example had been filled with paradox. On the one hand, he went around alleviating suffering; on the other hand, he died in suffering obedience to his father's will.

On the one hand, he went around healing the sick, the incurable, the sinners; on the other, he said that whoever did not take up his cross was not worthy of him.

There were those who saw Jesus as healer, a liberator, and in following him they fought all types of disease, systematic oppression and evil, but as the human race increasingly tried to overcome suffering, new forms of suffering were irrevocably created.

I did not believe for a moment that there were any "solutions" that would once and for all stamp out every kind of suffering. There was no way that "good systems" would eliminate all suffering, because there would always be people with bad motives to take advantage of good systems, just as there had always been people who had tried to humanize dehumanizing systems. For this reason, the question of human suffering and of God's part in it was very much on my mind.

I had already experienced a change when I discovered that God was not out there somewhere in the remote distance, the transcendent God, but She was also operating actively within me, the immanent God. Of course, I had always known about the God of Biblical history who enters into the history of men and women as they move forward toward the future.

My second big revelation came when I discovered in myself and others how much pain and agony there is involved in the task of caring and of leadership, when I realized to what lengths love must be prepared to go. So if God is love, then God's willingness to go to any length for love's sake can be no less than that of any human beings. It was this kind of love that manifested itself in Jesus.

I had come to believe that Jesus' life and dying had represented God's infinite and tender respect for human freedom, but I found that many still were trying to make the Cross into nothing more than a symbol of human guilt, and this they had done by absolutizing some aspects of theological language and by disregarding others.

I believed that Jesus was the purest expression of God's compassion with human beings, regardless of those who were still trying to make him into a symbol of God's need for appeasement.

I knew that He had come to proclaim God's unconditional grace, thus making possible for human beings a new orientation, in spite of the fact that many were still making Him into a condition for grace.

I realized, too, that even if his death on the cross had been a token of how far God would go in his fight against human suffering and unfreedom, there would always be those who would make the same Cross into a justification for the dumb endurance of suffering and unfreedom. I knew that there would always be the danger of absolutizing some aspects of theological language. I had known other aspects of it, however, and I wanted to use these to put down my experience.

If I believed it to be true that Jesus suffered for our sins, I knew that he also suffered because of our stumbling freedoms, our painstaking process of growing into maturity, because of the extraordinary challenges to our human limitations that we have to face. I believe that he was put to death because he knew of his Abba's unshakeable faith in us; because he knew that God would never turn Her back on creation.

There was no way in which we could be free if we had to live our lives according to some predetermined blueprint defined by a thousand oughts and shoulds. There was, also, no way in which we could be free if we got lost in our own mistakes and the power of evil. So, as we were to seek out our individual and collective destiny in freedom, we were also assured of the patient forbearance and compassion of God. And the reason that we know this is because this freedom, compassion, and patient forbearance of God took shape in Jesus.

I believed that God loved the world in this way. That is why I chose to write my thesis on the Crucified God of Jürgen Moltmann. In his theology of the Cross, I could find the language that would do justice to my experience of God.

The final product had to be judged by one United Church theologian, one Presbyterian, and a Catholic one. It took them awhile to agree on what should go into it, but in the end they did agree in their recommendation that my final draft be accepted as part of the requirement of an M.A in theology.

* * *

A hush fell over the crowd when the first faculty members leading the procession of graduands appeared in the doorway of the vestry. We had gathered in the basement of the Cathedral, sorting through gowns and stoles of various colors, each designating the discipline or faculty to which one belonged and the type of degree attained. At first I had felt ill-at-ease, because I had been farming long and hard that summer, and only a few weeks ago I had received notice that my thesis had been accepted so that I would graduate this fall. However, my uneasiness was short-lived. Harold, my thesis advisor, a United Church theologian and father of five, plopped down beside me, and we got caught up in an animated conversation.

"Why don't you become a United Church minister," he said, his eyes on a silk fuchsia shoe peeping out from underneath my black graduation gown. The shoes were a left-over from my daughter's wedding.

"I have changed cultures once already; I am not about to do it again," I replied dryly, while chewing on the tip of my finger.

Besides, I wasn't looking for a job. Sixteen hours a day, seven days a week for the last six months had been enough for me.

We had lined up in rows and now we walked down the aisle of the church where we were to receive our degree, first the doctorates, then M.A.'s of all sorts and the M.Div.'s. The M. Div.'s were conferred upon those who had spent three years preparing for active ministry, and they by far outnumbered all the others.

I was too nervous to feel very much, in spite of my friendship with Harold and the presence of a few familiar faces, Mary's being one of them. I was proud of them, all these men and women who represented a true renaissance in theological thought, yet, all the while, I wondered why I did not feel some great surge of inner radiance and joy, some passion, some excitement.

It was a proud moment, but I felt I was seizing it angrily: let no one take this one proud moment away from me.

I was angry because I could just as well not have made it.
I felt that I had been fighting for my very life.
And I was surprised at myself that I had done it.

But the journey had been as rich as its destiny. To be a pilgrim was just as rewarding as getting to the promised land.

The happiness had lain in the striving, in the discipline, in the goal.

At the reception, I was once again myself, making humorous remarks, smiling at the right time and looking composed and confident when I was expected to. Daniel was there, too. He was only just recovering from a broken leg, and he was hopping around with the help of a cane. He chatted unrestrainedly with professors and graduates alike. He had always been more of a people's person than I was. His world, after all, was straightforward and unambiguous. The learned theologians were charmed by his sincerity, his artlessness. Perhaps the farmer in him was giving them thoughts of the earth, the animals, the closeness to nature, things that they had left behind along with their childhood, and to which they now looked sometimes as to a paradise lost. Little did they appreciate that farming, too, had become a demanding, exacting profession.

While Daniel was mixing happily with the crowd, I fortified my social skills with wine, cheese, and sausage rolls. If being Belgian and Canadian simultaneously had once made me seem like an enigma to many people, being a farmer with a master's degree in theology only increased their puzzlement.

The reception over, we continued to celebrate in a room at a hotel near the airport. There, Mary and her husband joined Daniel and myself to rehash the day's events over a bottle of champagne. Daniel and I had planned this day to be somewhat of a holiday; it hadn't exactly turned out that way, but what the hell, every fall we had found ourselves to be exhausted and broke. Nothing had changed.

All evening long, I could see planes landing at Pearson International airport, one after the other. Their wings, like mine, seemed to droop from the long journey. I reflected how those same wings had carried me, often, from one country to another. At those times, I had often wondered what the future had in store for me. I wondered now.

All I knew was that, from there, Mary would go to her new job as a Retreat Center Coordinator, and I would return home to year-end statements, unpaid bills, and musical maternity pens where new calves where being born at the tune of five a week.

True, on the outside, nothing had changed. On the inside, however, everything had changed. I had changed.

Somewhere, I would find the time to work on a degree in Family and Marriage therapy.

Then, I would start to write a book.

Notes

1. M. Scott Peck, *The Road Less Travelled: A New Psychology of Love, Traditional Values and Spiritual Growth* (New York: Simon & Schuster, 1978), p. 97.

2. From Neil Diamond's song, "Sweet Carolyn."

3. The term 'limerence' (sometimes spelled 'limerance') was coined by Dorothy Tennov. "To be in a state of limerence is to feel what is usually termed 'being in love'." (Dorothy Tennov, *Love and Limerence: The Experience of Being in Love* (New York: Stein & Day, 1979) p. 16. David and Joyce Rice in *Living Through Divorce* also prefer to use this word when they speak about an obsession with the experience of being in love.

4. M. Scott Peck, *The Road Less Travelled,* describes the danger of such myths in some detail, pp. 91-97.

5. St. Paul's Epistle to the Hebrews, 12:5-7.

6. T.S. Eliot, from "East Coker."

7. Mary Giles, ed. *The Feminist Mystic, And Other Essays on Women and Spirituality* (New York: Crossroad, 1982), p. 96.

8. Bette Middler from "The Rose."

9. "The contrast between perfection as lack of darkness, and perfection as completion, meaning inclusion of darkness in a paradoxical whole, is a subtle, but vastly important concept of psychotherapy." John A. Sanford, in *Dreams: God's Forgotten Language* (New York: J.B. Lippington Co., 1968), p. 88.

10. Dietrich Bonhöffer, *Verzet en Overgave* (Baarn: Ten Have, 1968). This excerpt is my own translation taken from the Flemish version by Valeer Deschacht in *Op Zoek naar Vrede,* (8520 Lauwe: Fiews en Quartier, p.v.b.a., 1984), p. 20.

11. Joy K. Rice & David G. Rice, *Living Through Divorce, a Developmental Approach to Divorce Therapy* (New York: Guilford Press, 1986), p. 60.

12. Jean Vanier, from *Tears of Silence* (Toronto: Griffin House, 1970), p. 10.

13. "Sarah and the Seaplanes," *Ladies Home Journal,* Feb., 1949.

14. Maslow, Abraham H., *Toward a Psychology of Being* (New York: D. Van Nostrand Company, 1968), p. 201.

15. *The Road Less Travelled* has a chapter entitled "Love and Psychotherapy," which deals extensively with this problem (pp. 169-180).

16. I am indepted to Scott Peck and the Chapter on "Grace," in *The Road Less Travelled,* for helping me name this experience of grace and the miracle of health apart from observable causes.

17. Alfred Adler, *The Individual Psychology of Alfred Adler,* ed. by Heinz and Rowena Ansbacher (New York: Basic Books, 1956), p. 353.

18. This was the main concern expressed by Tom Harper in his lecture to the students of W.L.U. in January, 1987, but the experience of having one's creativity stifled for the sake of conformity is common to people of deep and genuine faith in every religion.

19. Edwin Friedman in *Generation to Generation, Family Process in Church and Synagogue* (New York: Guilford Press, 1985) argues the importance of such self-definition as a quality of leadership in one's family or Church.

20. Louis-Albert Vachon, Archbishop of Quebec and primate of Canada, speaking on male-female reconciliation in the Church, as quoted by Remi De Roo at the Washington Conference on Women in the Church.

21. Mary Malone makes this point very strongly in an article entitled, "The Case for Ordination," *Grail*, Vol. 4:2, 1988.

22. Carol P. Christ, *Diving Deep and Surfacing, Women Writers on Spiritual Quest* (Boston: Beacon Press, 1986), p. 23.